HOW TO TEACH
BIBLE STORIES

HOW TO TEACH BIBLE STORIES

Mary Nelson Keithahn
Marilyn H. Dunshee

Abingdon
Nashville

HOW TO TEACH BIBLE STORIES

Copyright © 1978 by Abingdon

Second Printing 1979

Library of Congress Cataloging in Publication Data

Keithahn, Mary Nelson, 1934-
   How to teach Bible stories.

   Cover title: How to teach Bible stories to children.
Bibliography: p.
   1. Bible stories--Study and teaching. 2. Christian
education--Teaching methods. I. Dunshee, Marilyn,
1923-   joint author. II. Title. III. Title: How
to teach Bible stories to children.
BS546.D86   268'.6   78-8714

ISBN 0-687-17960-2

The idea for the Map Board Game on page 36 originated
with Sonja Anderson from St. Luke's Presbyterian
Church, Wayzata, Minnesota, and is used with her
permission.

The idea for the Word Game on page 54 was adapted from
an experience Mary Ellen Beard of Essex Junction,
Vermont, described in the August, 1972, issue of
JED Share.

The use of the Pick-a-Picture Box on page 62 was
first developed by Donald L. Griggs, Director of
Continuing Education at the Presbyterian School of
Christian Education in Richmond, Virginia.

The scripture quotations in this publication are
from the Revised Standard Version Common Bible,
copyrighted © 1973.

MANUFACTURED BY THE PARTHENON PRESS AT
NASHVILLE, TENNESSEE, UNITED STATES OF AMERICA

Contents

Preface

There's more to learning a Bible story than hearing it!

Although most of us who teach Bible stories to students in our churches would not argue with this statement, our methods too often seem to contradict it. We are good at telling a story, but forget that hearing a story is only a first step in learning it. Our students need to have a variety of experiences with a story in order to discover its meaning and relate it to their lives.

The purpose of this book is twofold. First, it lists sixteen different categories of experiences that can help students learn a Bible story. Second, it suggests a variety of teaching-learning activities possible within each category. It should be noted that teachers should not try to use all sixteen categories of experiences to teach each Bible story to every group of students. Rather, they should be selective, choosing only those categories that are relevant to the age of their students and the content of their curriculum. Teaching-learning activities should be planned in terms of the resources, space, time, and leadership available.

This book is intended not to replace church school curricula but to help teachers learn to use their own curriculum resources more effectively and to supplement them with additional teaching-learning activities.

The book brings together the teaching-learning experiences of many church teachers who have helped one another grow in their ability to teach creatively. It was originally designed for the Minnesota Conference of the United Church of Christ to use in the 1976 Workshop Weekend, a training event for local church teachers held simultaneously at a number of different locations. Churches who would like to introduce this book to their teachers may want to consider a similar workshop plan that is described in the Appendix.

Where Is It?

Students need to learn how to find a story in the Bible. In what book is it found? Is that part of the Old or the New Testament? Does the story fill the whole book or a chapter or just a few verses? Once they locate the story, will they be able to find it again?

BIBLE LIBRARY CHART

To help students learn how to use the Bible, post a chart that shows the books of the Bible arranged on shelves according to types of literature. The chart emphasizes that the Bible is a library of books, that the books can be classified into different kinds of writings, and that they appear in a definite order.

Here's How:

1. Draw a Bible Library Bookcase on posterboard, using different colors to designate classification.
2. Write the names of the categories on the appropriate shelves and label each book as follows:

Old Testament
Law -- Genesis, Exodus, Leviticus, Numbers, Deuteronomy

History -- Joshua, Judges, Ruth, I & II Samuel, I & II Kings, I & II Chronicles, Ezra, Nehemiah, Esther

Poetry -- Job, Psalms, Proverbs, Ecclesiastes, Song of Solomon

Prophets -- Isaiah, Jeremiah, Lamentations, Ezekiel, Daniel, Hosea, Joel, Amos, Obadiah, Jonah, Micah, Nahum, Habukkuk, Zephaniah, Haggai, Zechariah, Malachi

New Testament
Gospels -- Matthew, Mark, Luke, John

History -- Acts

Paul's Letters -- Romans, I & II Corinthians, Galatians, Ephesians, Philippians, Colossians, I & II Thessalonians, I & II Timothy, Titus, Philemon

Other Letters -- Hebrews; James; I & II Peter; I, II, & III John; Jude

Prophecy -- Revelation

Try This:
1. Make an outline of a bookcase on flannel board and have flannel-backed, colored cardboard "books" that students can place in correct order.
2. Cover old cardboard blocks from the nursery or kindergarten room with colored, self-adhesive vinyl. With large letters, label the blocks with

the names of Bible books on one side. These then can be used in sets, individually, and in developing and playing games.

MARKED PASSAGES

In a learning center or in a class where students use Bibles from the church library instead of bringing their own, it may be wise to mark the passages they will be using in order to speed up the process of locating them.

Here's How:

1. Cut strips of construction paper or lightweight cardboard to bookmark size. Use a different color for each passage.
2. Write the Bible reference on each bookmark, and use it to mark the reference in the Bible.

SELF-INSTRUCTIONAL BIBLE STUDY

A set of four self-instructional workbooks designed to help students learn how to use the Bible and discover how it came to us is available. (See the Getting to Know Your Bible Series described in the Bibliography.) The format for each page is the same: new information, a question for the student to answer, and the answer to the question asked on the previous page. The books may be used by individuals at home or in class, or by the group under the direction of a teacher. Each student will need a copy.

These workbooks should be used to supplement, not replace, your curriculum. If used alone, the students will tire of the approach.

USING THE CONCORDANCE

The concordance is a tool every Bible student should learn to use. It is an alphabetical index of the principal words in a book, citing the passages (book, chapter, and verses) in which they occur. For example, a concordance may be used by persons who vaguely recall a phrase and want to find the exact quotation in which it appears or persons who want to find out what the Bible has to say about a given topic, word, or leading character.

A concordance may be found in some editions of the Bible, but it is also published separately.

What Is the Story?

Students need to become familiar with a story by experiencing it more than once, but not always the same way!

PICTURE-SCRIPTURE MATCH-UP

Students may be introduced to a story by reading portions of scripture and finding pictures to illustrate each one.

Here's How:

1. Assemble a variety of mounted pictures (from your curriculum resources, Sunday bulletins, calendars, magazines, or other sources) illustrating events in a story; for example, what happened during Holy Week or ways Jesus showed God's love to people. Lay the pictures on a table.
2. For each picture, select a brief scripture reference and write it on a card. Put the cards in a basket.
3. Ask each student to choose a card, find and read the reference in the Bible, and select a picture to illustrate it.
4. When all the students have completed this task, have them sit in a circle to share their pictures as you call out each reference in proper sequence.

Try This:
1. Have the students work in small groups to share their pictures through bulletin board displays developed around each. Symbols, words, other pictures, and decorative materials may be added as desired.
2. Correlate scripture references with headlines, news articles, and pictures from current magazines and newspapers. For example, some of Amos' prophecies about injustice could be matched with information on the problems of world hunger in the media. Mount each item or group of items separately. During the sharing time, ask the students to explain the reasons for their choices.
3. Obtain a set of Scripture Cards produced and sold by the American Bible Society (see Bibliography). The colored 4" x 7½" cards feature line drawings by Annie Vallotton from the Good News Bible on the one side and corresponding scripture passages on the other. Suggest that the students, using just the illustrated sides of the cards, choose pictures to match scripture references. Or use an overhead projector to enlarge the drawings to make posters for use in matching with scripture references. Posters for some of the cards are

available from the American Bible Society.

GUIDED BIBLE STUDY

Students may be helped to read a Bible story for themselves by using a cassette tape in a listening station in combination with a printed worksheet.

Here's How:

1. Prepare copies of a worksheet based on the story for each student. It could be a fill-in-the-blanks or matching exercise, a crossword puzzle, or any exercise designed to take the students through the story.
2. Provide Bibles for the students.
3. On a cassette tape for a listening station, record the following:
    a. A statement that the tape is to be used with the worksheet.
    b. Directions for finding the story in the Bible, with the request to stop the tape until all have found it.
    c. The Bible story, preferably read by another teacher or parent so there is a change of voice, with the request that the students follow along in their own Bibles.
    d. Directions for the worksheet, with the request to return to the tape when all have finished.
    e. The correct answers for the worksheet.
    f. Directions for rewinding the tape.

PRERECORDED STORIES

Teachers who find storytelling difficult may want to build up a library of prerecorded stories to use in listening stations or with the class as a whole.

Here's How:

1. Select the stories you want to use from your curriculum resources, the Bible, or Bible storybooks. Recruit a parent, older teen-ager, or someone else who is a good storyteller to record them for you on cassette tapes.
2. Choose relevant stories from those recorded commercially (see Bibliography). Transfer any 33 1/3 rpm recordings to cassette tape for easier use.

COSTUMED STORYTELLER

A Bible story becomes more real to students when told in the first person by someone who was a part of it.

Here's How:

1. Ask a parent, older teen-ager, or other adult with a flair for drama and storytelling to appear in class in costume, carrying a few simple props, to tell the story either as one of the characters or as someone who lived in that time.
2. Ask several persons to represent characters in the story and act out some scenes from it.

BIBLE STORYBOOKS

Children may be introduced to a Bible story through a well-illustrated collection of stories or a picture-book version of a single story.

Here's How:

1. Choose these books carefully, so that their retelling is faithful to the story in the Bible and the illustrations are worthy of the text.
2. If the children need help in reading the story for themselves, record the story on cassette tape with audible cues to indicate page-turnings. Use with a listening station in a learning center.
3. If you are reading or telling the story to the children, illustrate it with pictures from one or more of these books.

STORIES IN SONG

Students can become familiar with a Bible story by listening to songs based on that story, either live or recorded, and singing the songs themselves.

Here's How:

1. A number of musical dramas based on Bible stories for children and youth are available on commercial recordings. Use selected songs or the entire work to introduce the story. Other commercial albums may include individual songs or story-songs that can be used (see Bibliography). Transfer all or parts of the recordings to cassette tape for easier use.
2. Check denominational hymnals, children's hymnals, collections of folk songs and spirituals, and contemporary collections of religious songs based on Bible stories. Ask your children's choir director if there are any simple unison anthems based on Bible stories that you could use. As you introduce the story, sing the related song yourself or invite a musician from the congregation to sing it and teach it to the children.
3. Make up new texts to old tunes yourself to tell the story (folk songs and spirituals work well).

MULTIPLE CHOICE WORKSHEET

A series of statements with multiple choice endings can help students work through a story.

Here's How:

1. Paraphrase the story in a series of multiple choice statements.
2. For each statement, two of the choices should be obviously ridiculous, and the third obviously correct. The students will laugh at the alternatives and easily choose the right response, learning the story in the process.

SEE ALSO: *Check the Index for these related activities.*
Kamishibai Theater
Filmstrips, Filmslips, Films
Story Maze

What Do You See?

Students need to get a picture of the story in their minds. What do Bible lands look like? How did people dress? What kind of homes did they live in? How do artists think Jesus might have looked?

KAMISHIBAI THEATER

A Japanese-style portable box theater makes it easy for a storyteller to tell a Bible story while holding a series of pictures in clear view of the students.

Here's How:

1. Build a theater from a cardboard carton or wooden box. Cut out the back side, leaving a 1-inch border to act as a support. On the opposite, or front, side cut another opening ½ to 1 inch smaller than the size of your pictures. This is your stage. On the top of the box, near the stage opening, cut a narrow slit long enough for the pictures to slip into and wide enough to hold the whole set of pictures securely. The box should be slightly less in depth than the pictures so that their top edges will extend upward for

easy removal. Cut a second and similar slit in the top near the open back. Decorate the theater as desired.

2. Prepare your pictures, using teaching pictures from your curriculum, original drawings, pictures clipped from curriculum resources, or related contemporary magazine pictures, all mounted on posterboard cut to a given size. Number the pictures in proper sequence. Write the story line for each picture on separate pieces of paper, numbering them in proper sequence. Glue the story line for each picture to the back of the preceding picture; that is, the story line for #1 will be on the last picture, the story line for #2 will be on the back of #1, and so forth.

3. Place all the pictures in proper sequence in the front slit of the theater. You should be able to read the story lines through the opening in the back. After you have read the story line for the first picture, remove it, place it in the second slit, and read the caption on its back for the second picture. Continue in this way until all the pictures have been moved to the second slit and the story has been told.

slots

opening for pictures

opening in back so script can be read

Try This:
Use the kamishibai theater as a learning activity for your students. Enlist their help in constructing and decorating the theater. Encourage them to prepare sets of original drawings and stories based on Bible stories they have been learning; for example, the "lost" parables told by Jesus, Jesus' encounter with Zacchaeus, the Nativity stories, the story of Jonah.

BOOK ILLUSTRATIONS

Illustrations in picture-book versions of Bible stories and photographs in Bible background books can help students visualize a story in its setting. Younger students will be able to use the illustrations in books geared for older students if they are marked and a sentence explanation is given.
Sometimes you may want to use book illustrations with all of your students at one time. Unless the illustrations are of the large, picture-book size, this is difficult. Opaque projectors, which project the image of the illustration directly on the screen, are expensive and not readily available. There are other ways.

Here's How:

1. If the illustrations are drawings with simple lines and color, trace them on overhead transparencies so they can be projected while the story is read live or on cassette tape. Since the transparencies probably will be handled repeatedly, use permanent marking pens instead of the usual water-soluble projection pens that tend to smear easily.
2. Trace illustrations with simple lines and color onto overhead transparencies, using water-soluble projection pens. Project the transparencies onto large pieces of posterboard taped or held to the wall. Sketch the illustration in pencil on the posterboard. Color it in later with crayons and marking pens. Punch the posterboard illustrations at the top, fasten them together in sequence with notebook rings, and use them as a flip chart as you tell the story.
3. Ask a photographer in your congregation to photograph more complex pictures (e.g., paintings and photographs) so you can project them as colored slides.

MAGAZINE ILLUSTRATIONS

Magazines like National Geographic sometimes have beautiful color photographs relating to biblical geography, history, and culture. Teachers can use these illustrations in several ways to help students see the stories they are learning in their setting.

Here's How:

1. If the illustrations are printed on clay-base paper, you can lift the ink off the paper and transfer it to a transparency to be used with an overhead projector. (The colored inks used in printing are transparent.) The method is described in Better Media for Less Money, pp. 39-41 (see Bibliography).

19

2. Photograph the illustrations for projection as colored slides.

3. Mount the pictures for display as directed in Better Media for Less Money, pp. 27-36.

FILMSTRIPS, FILMSLIPS, FILMS

Audio-visuals can help students see a Bible story in their minds. Teachers can use audio-visuals in a variety of ways.

Here's How:

1. Divide students into listening teams, with each team given a certain thing to look and listen for while watching the audio-visual. Use their reports as the basis for a group discussion after the showing.

2. Divide the students so that one-fourth of the group are in one place and three-fourths are in another. Let the smaller group see the film without hearing the sound and the larger group hear the sound without seeing the film. Ask them to try to figure out what is happening and to take note of any questions they have while the film is in progress. After the showing, bring the students together to share their ideas of what the story was about. Then show the film again so all can see and hear it. Have them share their reactions to the story after this second experience. (This process helps students not only to see the story in their minds but also to reflect upon its meaning and communicate their ideas about it to one another.)

3. Show only enough of a film or filmstrip to give the students an idea of the conflicts or problems facing the characters in the story. Then stop and ask the students what they think will happen next. Provide opportunities for them to write, tell, act out, or draw the ending they select and time for them to

share their responses with the total group. Then show the rest of the film or filmstrip and compare its ending with the ones they suggested.

4. After the students have viewed a filmstrip with interesting sound effects, show it again without the recorded narration. Tell the story in your own words, and ask the students to provide the proper sound effects.

5. Since some students may be absent when an audio-visual is used and others may want to see it again, make it available for individual or small-group viewing during the next several class sessions. This will be possible if the audio-visual is part of your curriculum resources or church library, but less so if you have to rent it from a film library. Do not overlook the possibility of borrowing audio-visuals from churches of other denominations in your community.

STUDENT-PRODUCED VISUALS

Learning activities in one classroom sometimes produce visual materials that can be used with students in other age groups or with future classes.

Here's How:

1. Photograph scenes from a story posed by children in costume before backdrops they have painted. Project the scenes as colored slides to tell the story to another class or motivate a similar project for them.

2. Photograph artwork (murals, banners, posters, drawings) to use in the same way. Or ask another group of students to write the story told by the artwork in their own words.

3. Use a clay lamp or paper-mache water jug made by students as props for dramatizing a story.

4. Have students share a puppet play or kamishibai story with another class.

5. Incorporate a student-made diorama of life in Bible times within a larger display.

TEACHING PICTURES

Teaching pictures are those sets of large pictures that are part of your printed curriculum resources or pictures of similar size obtained from art museums or other sources. Such pictures are designed more for group use than for use by individuals and are usually found in worship centers or on bulletin boards or display areas to illustrate stories and stimulate thinking about concepts. Teachers may also use the pictures in other ways to stimulate responses from the students.

Here's How:

1. Help students put themselves inside the picture by asking them to look at it carefully, select one person in it, and write what he or she might be thinking in prose or poetry. For example, fifth and sixth graders had studied the reactions of three groups of persons (Pharisees, sinners, and disciples) to Jesus. They were asked to pretend that they belonged to one of these groups and to write down how they felt about Jesus on paper cut in the shape of conversational balloons from a comic strip. Then the students looked at Duccio's painting Christ Healing the Blind, assigned their thoughts to various persons in the picture who were watching Jesus, and attached the conversational balloons accordingly. (If students had written poems, these could have been mounted and grouped around the picture, with colored yarn or ribbons connecting the poem with the person in the picture.)
2. On a bulletin board or magnetic board, display a group of pictures illustrating events from a story or stories about Jesus or another major biblical character such as David. On individual cards, write a description of the event and/or a biblical reference to it. Ask the students to match each description with the correct picture, using the biblical references as clues.
3. If you have an extra copy of a picture, make it into a jigsaw puzzle:
    a. Glue the picture to a cardboard backing with rubber cement. Cut apart as a jigsaw puzzle. Assemble it on a magnetic board, using kitchen magnets to hold the pieces in place.
    b. Glue the picture to a backing of felt or medium-weight nonwoven interfacing. Cut it apart as a jigsaw puzzle. Assemble it on a felt or flannel board.

TELEVISION PROGRAMS AND MOVIES

In checking television programs for a Sunday morning, or for another time, you may discover a Bible story production you would like your class to see. Puzzle symbols may be used as discussion starters following the viewing.

Here's How:

1. Draw simple symbols on lightweight cardboard. (Your students may relate a symbol to an incident more quickly than you, so don't hesitate to use general symbols like the butterfly, circle, scales of justice, cross, flower, or worm.) Cut each symbol into pieces as for a jigsaw puzzle, and put the pieces into an envelope.
2. For each puzzle symbol, write out a few questions for discussion. For example, these questions could be used with the butterfly symbol:
    What does the butterfly symbolize?
    How does this symbol relate to parts of the film?
    What does the symbol have to do with your feelings at the end of the story?
Include a set of questions with the puzzle symbol in each envelope.

3. View the program with your students.

4. Divide the class into groups of three or four. Give each group an envelope. Have them put the puzzle together, and then discuss the symbol in relationship to the story, using the set of questions included in the envelope as a guide.

5. Have the groups share their symbols and results of their discussion with the total group.

Try This:
This approach may also be used with commercially produced films.

SEE ALSO:
Model Scenes

Who Plays What?

Students need to be able to identify the characters in a story and the roles they play. Don't forget that in any Bible story, God usually has one of the leading roles!

WHO AM I?

Riddles about characters in a Bible story can help students remember their names and their roles in the story.

Here's How:

1. Choose some characters from the story and decide what you want the students to remember about each.
2. Make up a riddle about each one in a sentence or a catchy rhyme. For example:
   I'm not very tall, so I climbed a tree.
   Jesus was coming, and I wanted to see. (ZACCHAEUS)
3. Write or type the riddle on one side of a 3" x 5" card and the answer on the other side. Students can use the riddles alone, with a friend in a learning center, or in free moments before or during class.

Try This:
Invite the students to make up their own riddles about people they have met through Bible stories.

REBUS POSTER PUZZLES

A rebus is a riddle made up of pictures of objects or symbols whose names sound like a word or syllables of a word. Rebus puzzles in the form of posters can be made up for characters in a Bible story. For example:
   A picture of a girl holding a drawing she had made with the caption "This is Ann." (ANDREW, a disciple of Jesus)
   A pair of jeans (cut from denim, with the pockets, fly, and belt stitched by machine, followed by "-S." (LEVI, Joseph's brother)
   A "D" cut from wallpaper, followed by "+ another word for the high school yearbook." (DANIEL, the prophet)

Here's How:

1. Choose the characters from the story for the puzzles. Consider the different ways you could give clues for their names or syllables in their names.

2. Use 11" x 14" pieces of poster-board for the posters. For illustrations, use permanent marking pens for drawings, letters, and words; magazine pictures and letters; and collage materials of all kinds. Afix materials to the posterboard with rubber cement, using the method described in Better Media for Less Money, pp. 27-28 (see Bibliography).

WHO ARE WE? A GAME OF PAIRS

Sometimes persons in a story can be paired together because they have something in common. These pairs can be used as the basis for a game to help students identify these persons and their relationship to one another.

Here's How:

1. List the names of persons in the story who can be paired together because they have something in common. Names may be used more than once, since persons may have different things in common with different people. Write the names of each pair on blank playing cards or posterboard cards, using permanent marking pens.
2. For each pair, write a descriptive clue on another card.
3. To play the game, the students work alone or in pairs to match each pair correctly with its description.

Try This:
1. This game works well with characters from the story of David. For example:
   A prophet and his king (NATHAN AND DAVID)
   A father and his son (SAUL AND JONATHAN)
   Two friends (JONATHAN AND DAVID)
   A soldier and his wife (URIAH AND BATHSHEBA)
   Two kings (SAUL AND DAVID)
   A loving father and a rebellious son (DAVID AND ABSALOM)

2. This game could also be used as the basis for a printed worksheet.

PUPPET PARADE

Making life-size, half-figure stick puppets of characters from Bible stories helps them come alive for children.

Here's How:

1. Make a list of characters in a Bible story. Let the children, working alone or in pairs, choose which they will portray as puppets.
2. Provide a variety of pictures, illustrated books, and a Bible dictionary or encyclopedia for the students to use in researching their characters. They will need to know when they lived and where, their work, the kind of clothing they would have worn, and so forth. The students should write the name of their puppets and a short description of them on 3" x 5" cards that can be glued to the base of the puppets when they are finished.
3. Each puppet will require a piece of cardboard approximately 2' x 3'. Ask your local hardware, appliance, or furniture stores for empty card-board cartons. Cut out the basic puppet shapes ahead of time, using a utility knife (available from hardware stores) and this pattern, enlarged to proper size.
4. Provide a variety of materials for dressing the puppets: wallpaper samples, construction paper, yarn, bits of lace and other trims, fringe, braid, ribbon, buttons, paper doilies, fabric scraps, tissue paper, colored marking pens, crayons, and so on. Have scissors, pencils, and glue ready. Pour white glue into a container with a plastic lid (so it can be covered when not in use), and thin with a little water so it can be applied with a small paint brush.

(Be sure to have the students wash
the brushes thoroughly after each
use.) Roll a rubber brayer over the
puppet to ensure a more permanent
bond between the glued-on materials
and the backing.

5. On the backs of the finished
puppets, help the students fasten
securely 3/4-inch dowel sticks with
masking tape.

6. The puppets are now ready to be
paraded through the classroom, into
the sanctuary for a worship service,
or into the fellowship hall for a
sharing time. Encourage the students to introduce their puppets and
tell something about them. Provide
a place where they can post their
puppets like flags in a flagpole
(e.g., 2" x 8" boards with holes
drilled to receive the dowels) so
they can be admired.

WALKING BIBLE FOLK

Bible characters can become very
special to students if they choose
certain ones to study and research
and then share them with others by
becoming Walking Bible Folk.

Here's How:

1. Make a list of characters from
which the students can choose. Provide Bibles and Bible reference books
for them to use in researching the
characters.

2. Obtain empty cardboard cartons
from grocery, appliance, hardware, or
furniture stores. The cartons should
be large enough so the students can
fit inside them and be covered from
the top of their heads to just above
their knees. Also, gather these
materials: latex or poster paint,
1-inch brushes, wallpaper, cloth,
chalk, gummed tape, stapler, utility
knife, 1/4-inch dowels, old pieces of
sheets.

3. Fit the boxes on the students,
marking their shoulder heights on the
backs and fronts of the boxes, and
the lengths of their arms on the sides.
Dismantle the boxes and lay them flat
to work on. Cut handholds on the
sides where marked. (This will help
the students steady the boxes as they
walk.) At the shoulder-height mark-
ings on the back and front of each
box, cut opening large enough to receive the 1/4-inch dowels. For each
box, cut two pieces of dowels 2 inches
longer than the width of the box. Pad
these with sheets, and fasten them inside the box at shoulder height by
inserting them into the openings you
have cut. (The dowels will allow the
boxes to rest on the students' shoulders.) Finally, cut out small eye-
holes on the front of the box in the
head area.

4. Encourage the students to dress
their character with paint, wallpaper,
fabrics, and other materials.

5. Have the Walking Bible Folk parade
through church school classes. Have
them participate in a church service,
wearing a big name tag and being
ready to share something about their
character. Ask another class to invite them to their session as Mystery

Guests (discussed at the end of this chapter).

Try This:
1. Let the children keep their own heads for the costumes, using make-up, masks, or headpieces to disguise their identity. Cut holes in the tops of the boxes so the costumes will fit over their heads. Omit the dowels.
2. Since the box costumes should end just above the knees to enable the students to walk freely, students who want longer costumes could attach fabric or crepe paper to the bottom of the boxes to extend their length.

RUMMY

A simplified version of the game of Rummy, using a teacher-prepared deck of playing cards, can help students learn the names of biblical characters and some facts about them.

Here's How:

1. Make a list of twenty persons in a Bible story or group of stories. For example, if the students have been dealing with stories about the early church, based on the book of Acts, you might list: Peter, Stephen, James, Paul, Philip, Cornelius, Tabitha (Dorcas), John Mark, Lydia, Priscilla, Aquila, Silas, Barnabas, Timothy, Lois, Eunice, Eutychus, Ananias, Apollos, Festus, Agrippa.
2. Using commercially produced blank playing cards (see Bibliography) and permanent marking pens, make three cards for each person. At the top of each card write the person's name. Below write a fact about that person, using a different fact for each of the three cards. (The Bible stories and a Bible dictionary or encyclopedia will give you the information you need.) For example:

<u>Lydia</u>	<u>Lydia</u>	<u>Lydia</u>
a wealthy businesswoman who lived in Philippi.	was baptized with her household by Paul.	invited Paul and his friends to stay in her home.

3. Have the students play the game as follows: Shuffle the cards. If two or three are playing, deal out nine cards per person; if four to six are playing, deal out six cards each. Lay the other cards face down in a pile in the center of the table. This is the draw pile. Take the top card off the pile and lay it beside it, face up. This is the discard pile. Beginning with the player to the right of the dealer, the players take turns drawing one card at a time from the draw pile or the discard pile. (Since the cards in the discard pile are always face up, players may draw any one at any time, not just the top one.) If they keep the card drawn, they must discard one from their hand. The object of the game is to meld, or match up the cards in sets of three (all the cards for one suit or person). No players lay down any cards until one person is able to lay down complete sets. That person calls "rummy" to announce the game is ended and is declared the winner after reading the information on the cards in the matched sets. The cards should be reshuffled before another hand is played.

OLD MAID GAMES

Old Maid is a commercially produced card game involving pairs of cards and one odd card. The cards are shuffled and dealt out to all the players. The players lay down matching pairs from their hands and then take turns drawing from one another's hands until all the cards are paired up and laid down. The player holding the odd card loses the game.
Teachers can prepare Old Maid games to help students identify and remember characters from a Bible story.

26

Here's How:

1. For the cards, use commercially produced blank playing cards (see Bibliography) or cut pieces of light-weight posterboard or cardboard to uniform size and glue on wallpaper backing with rubber cement.

2. Choose at least sixteen characters from the story, including one that can be the odd card. Except for the odd person, make two cards for each character. Write the name of the person at the top of the card and a fact about the person's role in the story underneath. Use a different fact for each card. Illustrate with symbols or other relevant drawings, if desired. Use permanent marking pens so the writing and illustrations won't smear when handled repeatedly.

Try This:

1. For Disciple's Old Maid, use Judas for the odd card and, in addition to the other eleven disciples, add the names of these women who followed Jesus: Mary Magdalene, Salome (mother of James and John), Martha and Mary (sisters of Lazarus), Susanna, and Joanna.

2. If there aren't enough characters in a story for the game, include symbols for events in which the characters were involved. For example, an Old Maid game for the story of the Exodus could use Pharoah for the odd card, the characters of Moses, Aaron, Jethro, Joshua, Miriam, and Zipporah, and symbols for the golden calf, the Ten Commandments, the plagues, the burning bush, the crossing of the sea, water and manna in the wilderness, and so forth.

3. If you want to make up an Old Maid game for a story without a villain, let the characters take turns being the odd card. Make up two cards for each character, but alternate by removing one of a pair for each hand. The player holding the odd card at the

end of the game can be asked to share something about that character. In this way, attention can be focused on a different character for each hand.

BIBLICAL SIMULATION GAMES

Simulation games are games that involve persons in make-believe situations from past, present, or future life. Unlike real life, simulated situations are limited by time, space, and the persons in a given class or group. Nevertheless, such real-life elements as choice, chance, issues, feelings, values, and value conflicts are present. Participants in a simulation game are thus enabled to identify with the problems, feelings, and decisions facing persons in the real-life situations, reflect upon them, and learn from them.

Simulation games can be developed around situations in the Bible. A number of such games are available from commercial sources (see Bibliography under Griggs Educational Service). Teachers may also develop their own games.

Here's How:

1. From your curriculum resources, choose a biblical situation where it is important for the students to identify with the characters in terms of their problems, feelings, and decisions. For example, when students are studying the prophet Amos, you could develop a simulation game around the situation in Bethel at that time.

2. If your class is large enough, recruit a group of students to help you plan the game, either at a special session or in a room away from the rest of the class. Otherwise, ask older teen-agers, parents, or others in the church to help you plan ahead of time and assist in directing the game.

3. Use a filmstrip, story, or other

resources to acquaint the planning group with the situation; for example, injustice in Israel. Ask them to watch for illustrations of the situation that could be used in the game. For example, the group might decide to re-create the marketplace in Bethel, setting up places for a judge by the city gate, moneylenders, a grain merchant, a seller of sandals, and a landowner. They should plan who will play each role, who can bring props (e.g., hanging scales and dried peas or rice for the grain merchant), what signs will be needed, what costumes to wear, and how to arrange the room. One area of the room should be designated as the Temple, with a golden calf (a cardboard cut-out sprayed gold) there to symbolize the way the Israelites had begun to worship other gods.

4. Involve the planning group in helping to develop the rules for the game. For example, in this game on Amos, biblical name tags should be made for the players, coded by color or the first letter, so the merchants will know who are poor and who are rich. Most players should be poor. Money (paper play money or construction paper coins) should be counted out ahead of time for each player, making sure that the rich get more than the poor. In addition, each player will need a set of instruction cards to be followed in any order except where indicated:

  --Go to the grain merchant. Buy some grain for flour or some peas or beans for making soup.
  --Go to Benjamin's Bazaar. Buy a new pair of sandals.
  --The rent on your farm is due. Pick up your sacks of grain at the game director's table and take them to the landowner. Pay what is asked.
  --You do not have enough money for your taxes. Borrow $500 from the moneylenders.
  --You can't repay your debt to the moneylenders. Tell them you cannot pay, but will work hard to repay the money as soon as you can.
  --Keep this card until strangers appear in the marketplace. Stop what you are doing and watch them.
  --Keep this card until the merchants in the marketplace close their shops and go to the Temple. Go along and worship with them.
  --Keep this card in case you have any problems in the marketplace. If you are treated unfairly, take your complaint to the judge at the city gate. You may use this card more than once.

The merchants will need additional money for making change. The game director should have sacks of grain cut from construction paper (five per player.) The grain merchant will need paper sacks to package his grain.

The planning group should also make out instruction cards for those who will lead the game:

Merchant -- Watch the biblical name tags so you will know which players are poor. Charge the poor more than the rich. Give the poor false weights of grain. Bribe the judge to decide for you if the poor complain to him. When the game director signals you, close up shop and lead the others to worship in the Temple. Read Psalm 9:1-2 there. When Amos appears to utter his prophecy against neighboring countries, applaud and smile. When he speaks against Israel, act very angry.

Moneylender -- Charge the poor whatever high rate of interest the planning group decides. If the poor can't pay, sell them to the landowner as slaves. When the merchant goes to the Temple to pray, go along. When Amos appears to utter his prophecy against neighboring countries, applaud and smile. When he speaks against Israel, act very angry.

Judge -- Whenever the poor complain to you that they have been cheated by the rich, let it be known that you are open to a bribe. Decide for the rich as soon as they pay the bribe. When the merchant goes to the Temple to pray, go along. When Amos appears to utter his prophecy against neighboring countries, applaud and smile. When he speaks against Israel, act very angry.

Amos -- After the merchant reads Psalm 9:1-2 to the others in the Temple, storm into the area uttering portions of your prophecy, first against neighboring countries (Amos 1:11) while all the merchants nod and applaud, and then against Israel (2:6-7, 10-11; 3:2, 13-15; 4:1-2; 5:21-24). This will provoke an angry response from the others. Listen when Amaziah threatens you (7:12) and then reply with Amos 7:14-15. Repeat Amos 3:1-2, and then leave.

Amaziah -- After Amos utters his prophecy in the Temple and the others show their disapproval, threaten him with Amos 7:12.

5. Have the planning group list some questions to help the players reflect upon the simulation game. For example: What was happening to people in the marketplace in Bethel? How did you feel while you were playing the game? Did it make any difference if you were rich or poor? Why was Amos so angry? How did you feel about his criticism of the people in Bethel? Why? Where did Amos get his ideas and authority to speak? Why did he expect Israel to be better than other nations?

6. Suggest that the planning group follow up the simulation game by showing a filmstrip on Amos to the players and helping them look at the quotations from Amos more closely.

MYSTERY GUEST

Mystery guests from a Bible story or group of stories can add the element of surprise to a classroom. Let the students discover, through questioning, the names of the guests and their messages or roles in the story.

Here's How:

1. Contact one or more adults to impersonate Bible characters from a story. Ask them to become very familiar with the characters' lives and roles in the story. Provide costumes for them to wear.

2. When you introduce the costumed guests to the class, explain that the students will have to discover their identity by asking questions that can only be answered by yes or no.

3. Depending on the number of guests, divide your class into small groups so they can rotate from guest to guest. Each group should ask questions until they discover the guests' identities or a time limit is up. (When a group correctly identifies a guest, they should keep this information secret.)

4. No longer mysteries, the guests can tell their stories in first person.

Try This:

1. If you have at least five mystery guests, individual students can question them, keeping their ideas to themselves. When they think they know who the mystery guests are, they can identify them to a teacher and receive a small pebble, kernel of corn, or button for each correct answer.

2. Instead of asking them to impersonate Bible characters, ask contemporary professional people (e.g., legislators, lawyers, doctors, teachers) from your congregation or other churches to be themselves as mystery guests. When they have been

identified by profession and as
Christian laypersons, ask them to share
their responses to contemporary issues
related to a Bible story (e.g., justice, bio-medical problems, ecology.)

SEE ALSO:
Personal Facts Relay
One or Both Relay Quiz
Self-Testing Media
Bible Baseball
Go Fish
Picture Lotto

When Did It Happen?

"Let's see. . . . Did Moses live before Joseph? When were the kingdoms united?" So many Bible events are remembered as just that -- events with no relation to time or other historical happenings. Students need to learn how to place a story in time and in relationship to other events.

TIME LINES

A time line is a visual aid for helping students see events in a historical sequence and in the evolution of the revelation of God. Introduce students to a time line by helping them make one that spans their lives from birth to the present. Show how the time line can be divided into years, and have them help you place important events in their lives on it: birth date, when they moved, death of a family member or pet, marriage of an older sister or brother, going to kindergarten, joining Scouts, and so on. Then proceed to a longer time line related to your unit of study, noting dates of other familiar historical events.

Here's How:

1. Use shelf paper, and encourage students to illustrate it with pic-tures, quotations, symbols, and words, as well as dates and characters.

2. If you don't have space to put up a long time line, or if you want variety, use those posts in your room. Make a band of paper to encircle the post. On it record, in pictures or words, a section of the time line. Add more sections until you have the whole time line recorded on the post.

3. Boxes of all sizes can be deco-rated with symbols, pictures, and so forth and stacked like a tower or kiosk. These boxes can be used in review-type games too.

4. Put up a wire or string for a time line. Mark each important date in your study on a clip clothespin with colored felt pens. Clip the clothespins to the time line in the proper order. On 3" x 5" cards write the events that happened on those dates, one per card. Mix them up and put them in a small box. Invite the students to see how quickly they can clip the events to the correct dates.

5. Draw only lines and dates on a shelf-paper time line, writing Bible characters, events, and key words on small cards (one-third of a 3" x 5" index card) instead. Ask the students to pin the cards in the correct spots, using the time line in Young Readers

Bible (see Bibliography) if help is needed. Use this activity to introduce or review a time line.

MODEL SCENES

Model scenes can help students discover that life for the people in Bible stories was different from life today because they lived long ago and in another land.
A model home or village can be set up ahead of time in the classroom area by the teacher, or it can be a learning activity for students who set up a scene based on their research.

Here's How:

1. If you have enough space, build a home in one corner of your classroom. Use cardboard from large cartons (e.g., refrigerator, stove) for the walls. Paint them in earth tones with latex paint. (Do not use tempera as it sheds when dry.) Raise part of the floor with boards and bricks. Paint a mural on a nearby wall to show the terrain and other buildings. If there is a post in the area, convert it into a palm tree with crepe paper and wire branches. Make simulated articles from that time: a water jug from paper-mache; an oil lamp from salt/cornstarch/flour clay; a mat woven from strips of rags on a homemade loom; a mezuzah from a farmer's matchbox. Prepare foods for a tasting table. Make charts to show facts about the climate, population, and other characteristics of the area in the time of the story. Have a costumed storyteller describe the life of people who might have lived in this home.
2. If you are limited in space, have the students build a tabletop village. Houses could be made from milk cartons cut down, covered with paper-mache, and painted. Real sand and the artificial grass used with model

railroads could cover the table. The children could bring toy animals from home and make clothespin figures to people the village. Or have children work individually or in pairs to make a diorama, or scene in a box.

THEN AND NOW POSTERS

Then and Now Posters can be prepared by the teacher to puzzle the students or planned by students to show what they have learned.

Here's How:

1. Collect pictures of articles used today, articles used in the time of the Bible story, and articles used in both times. (For example: an airplane, an oil lamp, and a pottery bowl.) Glue these in random fashion onto a piece of posterboard. Ask the students to identify which fall into each of the three categories.
2. The students could select pictures from a similar group to glue onto posterboard under one of three headings: Then, Now, Both.
3. Collect pictures of articles used in Bible times and now to meet a certain need (e.g., worship, music, baking, homes, clothing, light, transportation). Ask the students to use the pictures to make a series of Then and Now Posters, each contrasting biblical and contemporary ways of meeting a specific need.

PICTURE LINE

When there is little wall space for display in a classroom, try a picture line.

Here's How:

1. String a clothesline along a wall or across the corner of a room.
2. Use clip clothespins to fasten

pictures of events within a story or within a particular span of time to the line.

3. Make a game out of the picture line by mixing up the pictures out of order. Ask the students to arrange them in correct chronological sequence.

Try This:

Instead of clothesline, use a heavy wire. Attach pictures with bulldog clips, purchased from a stationery store.

CHRONOLOGY GAMES

When students have worked with a number of Bible stories, they may need help in learning when people lived in relationship to others. Teachers can make up chronology exercises for them.

Here's How:

1. On large cardboard cards, write the names of characters from the stories, one name per card. Invite each child to choose a card, and then ask the children to arrange themselves in chronological order without your help. Suggest that they can refer to time lines in a Bible dictionary or encyclopedia for help. After playing the game several times, the students will probably be able to arrange themselves in correct order easily without help.

2. This same exercise can be adapted for events from a story or group of stories.

ARCHEOLOGICAL DIG

Students who are learning about the discoveries archeologists have made about the life, people, and events of Bible lands and times will enjoy participating in a simulated archeological dig.

Here's How:

1. Find a site for the dig in a field, garden, or empty lot. Be sure to obtain permission for using it from the owner.

2. Bury modern artifacts in the site, leaving clues that will help students decide where and how to excavate the dig. For example, obtain some old clay flowerpots. Draw designs on them with colored marking pens and then break them. Bury the pieces. Other artifacts could be charred sticks from a fire, broken dishes, tin cans, bottles, tableware.

3. Schedule a special session of your class for the dig. Explain that you have found a site that could be excavated, and ask the students to list the tools they will need; for example, shovels in several sizes, garden trowels, old paint brushes, sieves, stakes, string, tape measure, notebooks, camera. Ask for volunteers to bring these things. Remind the students to wear old clothes and dress for the weather.

4. Follow archeological procedures for the dig, photographing each step as a record of the excavation. Have the students use stakes and string to lay the area out in grids. Map the area in a notebook, labeling each grid. As the students dig and uncover things, have them clean them off with brushes and record where they were found. When the buried artifacts have been recovered, replace the dirt and tidy the area.

5. Back in the classroom, have the students assemble broken dishes and pottery, using epoxy glue. Ask them to use these and the other artifacts to reconstruct the event that happened on the site.

6. Share the photographs and artifacts from the experience in a bulletin board display for the congregation.

Where Did It Happen?

Students need to locate a story in a place. Did the story happen in Palestine or Egypt or Babylonia or somewhere else? Were the characters out on the desert or near the river or on the sea? Was it hot or cold, wet or dry? How far was it from Jerusalem to Jericho?

WALL MAPS

Sometimes teachers wish that a map from an atlas or curriculum resource book could be enlarged for use on the wall or bulletin board. This can easily be accomplished with the use of an overhead projector.

Here's How:

1. Trace the map on an overhead transparency with water-soluble projection pens.
2. Use masking tape to fasten a large sheet of newsprint, posterboard, manila drawing paper, or wrapping paper on the wall.
3. Project the transparency map onto this paper. Trace the outlines with a pencil.
4. Take the map down and lay it on the floor or table. Go over the pencil

lines with permanent marking pens and add details. Color with crayons.

Try This:
1. Use the map as a reference for students as they complete a worksheet or other learning activity.
2. Let the students use the technique to make a map for the classroom themselves.

OVERHEAD TRANSPARENCY MAPS

Transferring a map from an atlas to an overhead transparency and projecting it in the classroom enables all the students to work with it together.

Here's How:

1. Use a permanent marking pen to trace a map from an atlas, Bible dictionary or encyclopedia, or curriculum resources onto a transparency. Label important places for your story and add color, as desired.
2. Cut out one side of an 8½" x 11" office file folder, leaving a 1-inch border around the edge to serve as a frame. Glue this over the transparency. When folded, the other side

of the folder will protect the transparency, and it can be easily stored.

Try This:

1. Use the transparency map in a learning center as a model for the students to use in completing a worksheet.

2. In a learning center, ask students to work with the map, using water-soluble pens to circle key cities (e.g., places where Jesus lived) or mark in journeys (e.g., the Exodus of the Hebrews from Egypt.) Provide resource books in the center for them to consult. When they have completed the task successfully, ask them to wash off the lines so the transparency will be ready for the next students.

3. Instead of making your own transparency map, use one of the commercially produced transparency sets (see Bibliography).

A TRIP MAP

When families plan a trip they often mark up a map as to beauty lookouts, historical spots, rest stops, campgrounds, relatives' and friends' homes. Why not take your students on a make-believe trip in Bible lands?

Here's How:

1. Remove all furniture from your classroom floor. If it is not washable, cover the floor with brown butcher paper.

2. Using tempera paints (with liquid detergent added to ensure washability), paint an enlarged outline map on the floor. Have the students help you label its important features, using an atlas or an overhead transparency map as a guide. Add pictures or symbols to represent events that happened at various places.

3. Then, as a group, go on a walk through the map to recall where the story events happened. Stop for a

date or fig snack and some cold water at an oasis.

4. You may want to provide mimeographed versions of the map for the children to record what they have learned and put in their class notebooks.

Try This:

Do not label or illustrate the map. Instead, have pictures, Bible quotations, place names, and events on 4" x 6" index cards. Mix and deal the cards to students until all the cards are used. As you travel around the map, stop at strategic points and have students identify cards that they hold with the rest area. Leave the cards there and move on along the trail to another area.

MAP RELAY

A relay is a pleasant way to test the students' knowledge of geographical features on a map.

Here's How:

1. Divide your students into two teams.

2. Post identical maps on the wall or bulletin board, one map for each team.

3. Position the teams equally distant from the maps, and give them these directions: As the name of a geographical feature is called out, each team should send up a member to locate it on the map. The first team to do so correctly scores a point. The game will continue until all the features have been identified. The team with the most points wins.

MAP BOARD GAME

A map can become the basis for a board game.

Here's How:

1. Make the board from a piece of posterboard 22" x 28." Glue a small map of Palestine in the time of Jesus in the center. Surround it with pictures (cut from bulletin covers, calendars, curriculum resources, etc.) illustrating events in the life of Jesus. Draw a 1½-inch border around the edge of the board. Divide it into small sections, labeling some with the names of places (color these green), some with bodies of water (color these blue), and some with the word "card" (color these yellow). Leave some sections blank.

2. Make a set of twenty cards, each one telling about some event in the life of Jesus from his birth to his resurrection. Number these in chronological order on the reverse side, from one to twenty. Provide one die.

3. Give these directions: The students move around the board according to the numbers they throw on the die. If they land on blue or green sections, they have to locate those geographical features on the map. If they land on a section labeled "card," they have to draw a card and read it aloud, putting it back under the pile when they have finished. The first one around the board wins the game.

SEE ALSO:
Model Scenes
Filmstrips, Filmslips, Films
Book Illustrations
Magazine Illustrations
Teaching Pictures

What Happened First?

Students need to be able to place the events of a story in proper sequence in order to understand and remember it. What happened first? What happened last? What happened in between?

WHICH CAME FIRST?

This game was designed to help students with the difficult task of putting events in a story in proper sequence.

Here's How:

1. Make a list of ten events from the story. Write each one separately on a 4-inch cardboard circle.
2. Use cloth tape to fasten together, end to end, ten 4" x 6" cards or pieces of posterboard. (This will enable you to fold up the sequence board like an accordion for storage.) Number each section in order from one to ten.
3. Explain to the students that they are to place the circles describing the events on the board in the order in which they happened. They may work alone or in pairs.

SEQUENTIAL CARDS

A set of cards illustrating events from a story can help nonreaders put those events in proper sequence.

Here's How:

1. Cut posterboard into squares or oblongs of equal size. Use permanent marking pens to draw illustrations of events in the story, one illustration per card. Simple line drawings or stick figures are adequate so long as they convey the story line. If drawing is difficult for you, ask a teenager or adult in the church to do it for you.
2. Ask the students to arrange the cards in the order of the events and then use them to retell the story in their own words.

Try This:
1. If you have a picture-book version of the story, ask a photographer in the church to photograph the illustrations and have prints made of each. Use these instead of the cards.
2. Use color slides of book illustrations, and have the students

arrange them in order on a slide
sorter.
  3. Here is a sample plan for
sequential cards on the story of
Joseph:
    Jacob gives Joseph the special
coat.
    Joseph, wearing it, tells his
brothers about his dreams.
    The brothers take Joseph's coat
and throw him in the pit.
    The brothers sell Joseph as a
slave.
    Joseph works as a slave in Egypt.
    Joseph, in prison, interprets the
dreams of another prisoner.
    Joseph is called to tell Pharoah
what his dreams meant.
    Pharoah thanks Joseph by making
him chief overseer.
    Joseph gives grain to his hungry
brothers from Canaan.
    Joseph welcomes and forgives his
brothers.

MATCH THE SYMBOLS WITH THE STORY

When events in a story can be
represented by symbols, the symbols
may become part of a matching exercise.

Here's How:

  1. Write brief descriptions of the
events in a story on pieces of lightweight posterboard cut to uniform size,
one event per card. Label these event
cards with letters of the alphabet.
  2. Use a permanent marking pen to
draw symbols for each event, one
symbol per card. Add color with other
pens or crayons. Number these symbol
cards in proper sequence.
  3. Glue medium-weight nonwoven interfacing on the backs of all the cards
so they will adhere to a felt board
or flannel board. (How to construct
a felt board is described in Better
Media for Less Money, p. 24, listed
in the Bibliography.)
  4. If you plan to use this exercise
in a learning center, make a key for
the students to use in checking their
answers.
  5. Ask the students to place the
symbol cards in order on the felt
board and then match up the events
with the appropriate symbols. If
they do this correctly, they will
have arranged the events in proper
sequence. Suggest that they check
their answers with the key and then
remove the cards from the felt board,
leaving them in scrambled order for
the next persons to use.

Try This:
  Matching Symbols and Events from the
Story of Moses
  1. Pyramids and head of Pharoah
    H. Although Moses was raised as a
prince in Egypt, he was angry about
the way his people, the Israelites,
were treated as slaves. One day he
killed an Egyptian overseer who was
beating a slave. Fearing Pharoah's
anger, he fled.
  2. Sheep or shepherd's crook
    C. Moses went to Midian, became a
shepherd, married, and had a family.
  3. Burning bush
    A. One day, while Moses was tending
his flocks, he saw a bush that seemed
to be burning, yet it was not consumed.
  4. Sandals
    F. Recognizing that he was in the
presence of God, Moses took off his
sandals in respect. God asked him
to go to Egypt and ask Pharoah to
free the Israelites so that they might
serve God.
  5. Flies and Frogs
    D. Pharoah refused until God sent
plagues on the Egytians. Finally,
when the eldest son in every Egyptian
family died, Pharoah let the Israelites go. Later he changed his mind,
and sent soldiers after them. But
God helped the Israelites escape.
  6. Bush with manna and a quail
    B. The people had to travel through
a great wilderness to reach the land
God had promised them. Often they

were discouraged and hungry, but God helped them to find food.

7. Stone tablets with Roman numerals up to ten

G. God also gave the people laws to help them learn how to act toward God and toward one another.

8. Golden calf

E. While Moses was away talking with God, the Israelites were afraid God had forgotten them. They persuaded Aaron to make a golden idol to worship. When Moses returned, he was angry with them, but asked God to forgive them. He knew the Israelites had much to learn before they would be ready to enter the new land.

RECONSTRUCTING A STORY

Sometimes students are more able to reconstruct a story when they can work with actual sentences from the story printed on individual cards.

Here's How:

1. Choose key sentences from a Bible story, or paraphrase it, keeping the story line intact. Write each sentence on a different card. Mix them up.

2. Using these sentences only, record the story on cassette tape for a listening station.

3. Give these directions: Create a continuous story by arranging these sentences according to your preference. When you have finished, listen to the story on the tape as told by someone who experienced this event.

Try This:

1. A Sample Story about Paul

Saul was threatening to murder the disciples of Jesus.

He went to the high priest and asked for a letter of introduction to the Jews in Damascus.

If he found any followers of Jesus, he was to bring them back to Jerusalem.

On the way to Damascus, a light flashed about Saul. Saul fell to the ground.

His companions heard a voice, but saw no one.

The voice asked, "Saul, why are you persecuting me?"

Saul answered, "Who are you?"

The voice said, "Go into the city, and you will be told what to do."

Saul could not see. He was blind!

Saul's friends led him into the city of Damascus.

A man named Ananias, living in Damascus, had a vision. The Lord told Ananias to go to Saul and heal him. Ananias was afraid because he was a follower of Jesus.

The Lord told Ananias that Saul would not hurt him, because he had chosen Saul to follow him and preach for him. Ananias healed Saul and told him the Lord's plan for him.

Saul was baptized.

Saul went to the synagogue and said, "Jesus is the Son of God."

2. If you have a filmstrip version of this story, show it without the accompanying narration, using instead the recorded reconstructed story.

3. Instead of writing the sentences on cards, mimeograph them on paper to be cut apart and pasted in proper order on a separate worksheet. If the sentences are short enough, use gummed labels to speed up the process.

SEE ALSO:

Story Maze

What Was That Again?

Students need to be able to recall specific facts from a story. What events happened? Who were the persons involved?

TIC-TAC-TOE

The game of Tic-Tac-Toe can be used to check the students' retention of factual information as well as their skill in a battle of wits.

Here's How:

1. Make a game board from a square of heavy cardboard (e.g., the packing from a phonograph record container). Divide it into nine equal squares with 3/4-inch wide colored plastic tape. Bind the edges with 1½-inch wide tape. Number the squares from one to nine.
2. For the game markers, cut five squares and five circles from poster-board in a size to fit within the squares of the game board.
3. On each of nine 3" x 5" cards, write a question about the story, putting the answer on the reverse side. Number the cards from one to nine. (Since the students may not choose the questions in numerical order, each question should be independent of the others.)
4. Give these directions: Two persons may play this game with a teacher in a learning center. The players take turns answering questions in order to get their markers on the board. One has squares, the other circles. The first player picks a numbered square, and the teacher asks the question with that number. A correct answer enables the player to put a marker on the square. An incorrect answer gives the other player a chance to answer the question. If successful, the second player puts a marker on the square and also has a chance to choose and try for another square. The first player to get markers on three squares in a row (across, down, diagonally) wins the game. If no person can win, the players take turns answering the remaining questions, and the one with the most correct answers is declared the winner.

Try This:
1. When Tic-Tac-Toe is played by two teams, use a game board made from a large square of colored posterboard.

Divide the board into nine equal squares. Cut ten smaller squares, five of one color and five of another. Draw an "X" on the first group, and an "O" on the second. Glue a small piece of Velcro fastener on the back of each and a matching piece in the center of each square on the board. The board can then be displayed on a bulletin board, and the markers easily fixed in place with the Velcro fasteners.

Write out a number of questions about Bible stories, characters, or events. (The number will depend on how many times you want to play the game.) Put the questions in a hat or box. Have the members on each team number off. Call one team X and the other O. Play as follows: Number 1 of X team draws a question. A correct answer allows that player to put an "X" in any square on the board, and number 1 of the O team has a chance to draw. An incorrect answer gives number 1 of O team a chance to answer it and, if correct, put an "O" on the board and yield to number 2 on O for a turn. If number 1 of O answers incorrectly, the turn reverts to number 2 on X team, and the unanswered question goes back in the hat. The first team to get three X's or three O's across or down or diagonally in a row is the winner.

2. Students themselves serve as markers in a version of the game called Human Tic-Tac-Toe. Mark off a Tic-Tac-Toe game board on the floor with masking tape. Each of the nine squares should be about 2 feet square or large enough for a student to stand in. Divide the students into two teams of at least five persons each. Label one team Circles and the other Squares. Team members can indicate their team by holding or wearing a sign or making body signals (arms crossed over their chest for squares, and arms held in front of their bodies with hands clasped for circles). The game is played as above, except that

as individuals take turns answering questions and give the right answers, they position themselves on the game board. If there are fewer than ten students in the class, make extra labels to use as stand-ins on the board as the game progresses.

3. Use a flannel board for the playing surface with ten flannel-backed cards for X's and O's.

4. A chalkboard can also be used for the game.

PERSONAL FACTS RELAY

When a unit includes stories about two or more major biblical characters, students sometimes need help in sorting out facts about each. This relay provides that help.

Here's How:

1. Select two or more characters who are important persons for the students to remember. Make sets of cards with biographical data for each, one fact per card. You will need a set for each team.

2. Divide the students into two or more teams. Give each team a set of cards that have been shuffled so the facts about one character are mixed up with those of the other.

3. Give these directions: at a given signal, the teams work to sort the cards into two groups, one for each character. The first team to do this correctly wins the relay.

Try This:
1. A Sample Relay on Peter and Paul

Facts About Peter--
-Was a fisherman on the sea of Galilee and lived in Capernaum
-Called by Jesus to be his disciple; one of the twelve closest to him
-Promised Jesus at the Last Supper that he would never betray or desert him, no matter what happened

-Was with Jesus when he went to pray
 in the Garden of Gethsemane before
 his arrest
-Was afraid for himself after Jesus
 was arrested, so denied knowing him
-Hid out with the other disciples
 after the Crucifixion because he
 was afraid for himself
-Was changed from a coward into a
 brave man when the risen Christ
 appeared to him, forgave him, and
 gave him a job to do
-Preached to people in Jerusalem at
 the time of Pentecost, at great danger
 to himself, and helped many people
 believe and be baptized
-Became a strong leader in the early
 Christian church.
-Met a man named Cornelius and became
 convinced that Gentiles who became
 Christians did not have to follow
 the Jewish laws
-Is thought to have been crucified
 upside down by the Romans as punishment for being a follower of Jesus

Facts About Paul--
-Came from Tarsus as a young Pharisee
 to study the Jewish law with famous
 rabbis in Jerusalem
-Watched the murder of a Christian
 leader, Stephen, by stoning
-Went on a mission to Damascus to
 persecute Jewish Christians in the
 synagogues there
-Had an experience with the risen
 Christ that changed his life
-Preached in Damascus that Jesus
 was the Son of God and all people
 should follow him
-Worked with people like Barnabas,
 Silas, Timothy, John Mark, Priscilla
 and Aquila, and Lydia
-Went on many missionary journeys to
 tell people in other cities about the
 Christian faith
-Was arrested in Jerusalem by the
 Roman officials after the Jews
 threatened his life for his belief
 that Gentiles who became Christians
 did not have to follow the Jewish laws

-Shipwrecked on way to Rome where, as
 a Roman citizen, he was sent for
 trial
-Wrote letters from prison to the
 people in the churches he had started
 to help them better understand Christian beliefs and actions
-Was probably beheaded by the Romans
 as punishment for being a follower
 of Jesus

2. Instead of two teams, two individuals could work with the sets of
cards in a learning center setting.
Or one person could work with a set
alone.

ONE OR BOTH RELAY QUIZ

Sometimes students can be helped to
remember facts about important biblical characters by having them compare
two related characters to see in what
ways they are alike and how they are
different.

Here's How:

1. Select two related characters from
a unit of study, such as Peter and
Paul. Write out twenty statements
that apply to one or both of the
characters.
2. Divide the students into two or
more teams. Give each team three
small cards: one for each of the
characters and one reading "both."
Ask the team members to group
together close enough so they will
be able to talk with one another
without the other team's hearing.
3. Give these directions: When the
leader reads a statement, each team
decides together whether it applies
to one or both of the characters and
puts the appropriate card (e.g.,
Peter, Paul, both) face down on the
table or floor. When the teams are
ready, they each turn up their cards
and the leader reads the correct
answer. A team adds a point for a

right answer and subtracts a point for a wrong answer. The team with the highest score at the end of the game wins.

Try This:
1. Use the statements about Peter and Paul from the previous section. Add these which apply to both:
--Put in prison because of his preaching
--Agreed that Gentiles who became Christians did not have to follow the Jewish law
--A Jew
--Was changed by his experience with the risen Christ
--Put to death in Rome, probably when the Christians were persecuted by the Roman emperor Nero
2. This game could be used also with two persons in a learning center setting.

QUICKIES

Review exercises can be fun, especially when they are in the form of a game that rewards correct answers with a chance to win bonus points for the team.

Here's How:

1. Make a list of twelve or more questions based on a story or group of stories. After each question, list a related but more difficult question as a bonus for those who answer the first question correctly.
2. Divide the students into two or more teams.
3. Give these directions: The leader asks one question at a time. The first team to have someone raise a hand gets a chance to answer the questions. Teams score one point for answering a question correctly, but subtract one point for a wrong answer. A correct answer to a bonus question is worth one point; there is no penalty

for a wrong answer. Teams should be encouraged to confer together before an answer is given. (It is also helpful to have one person judge whose hand is raised first and do the scoring and another read the questions.)

Try This:
Sample Quickies for the Exodus Story

1. Name of the book in the Bible where you find the story of Moses (EXODUS)
 Bonus: "Exodus" means ___(A GOING OUT)
2. Name of the agreement between God and the Hebrews or Israelites (COVENANT)
 Bonus: What is God's part? (PROMISING TO LOVE AND CARE FOR THE HEBREWS) What is the Hebrews' part? (OBEYING GOD)
3. Name of Moses' brother (AARON)
 Bonus: Names of Moses' sister (MIRIAM)
4. Number of commandments God gave the people through Moses (TEN)
 Bonus: Many years later Jesus summed these laws up in two commandments. What were they? (LOVE GOD AND LOVE YOUR NEIGHBOR)
5. A graven image is ____(AN IDOL OF WOOD, METAL, OR STONE)
 Bonus: The graven image the Hebrews made was in the shape of a ___(GOLDEN CALF)
6. A word for breaking the covenant and turning away from God (SIN)
 Bonus: Two ways the Hebrews sinned were____ (WORSHIPING THE GOLDEN CALF AND DOUBTING GOD'S LOVE WHEN THEY WERE IN THE WILDERNESS)
7. River in Egypt (NILE)
 Bonus: River in Canaan (JORDAN)
8. Leader of the Hebrews on the journey out of Egypt (MOSES)
 Bonus: Leader of the Hebrews on the journey into Canaan (JOSHUA)
9. A name for God (YAHWEH)
 Bonus: Another name for God (ELOHIM)
10. To want something someone else has so badly you'll do anything to get it (COVET)

Bonus: To tell a lie about someone in court (TO BEAR FALSE WITNESS)
11. To be unfaithful to your husband or wife (TO COMMIT ADULTERY)
Bonus: Holy means ____ (SET APART FOR A PURPOSE)
12. The holiday based on the Exodus event (PASSOVER)
Bonus: Easter always falls near Passover because ____ (JESUS' LAST VISIT TO JERUSALEM WAS TO CELEBRATE PASSOVER WITH HIS DISCIPLES)

FACTS POSTERS

Posters can be designed to highlight ideas, events, or people related to a Bible story. They can be made by teachers or students.

Here's How:

1. For each poster, use a 22" x 28" piece of posterboard. Use direct quotations, key words, flat pictures, drawings, three-dimensional materials, and so forth to illustrate ideas, events, or people related to a story.
2. Write a title for each poster on a small card.
3. Ask the students to match the title cards with the posters.

Try This:
Facts posters could be displayed individually when the related stories are told during the unit of study, and then used at the end of the unit as a review exercise.

SELF-TESTING MEDIA

Self-testing devices enable the students themselves to check their answers to review questions. They can be as simple as an answer key placed near a matching exercise in a learning center or as elaborate as an electric response board. They may be made by teachers or other adults in the congregation using materials that are inexpensive and readily available.

Here's How:

1. A Disc-a-Text is a self-testing device that can be made inexpensively from an ordinary file folder by cutting a window in each side of the folder and inserting a circle of posterboard with questions written on one side and answers on the other. When the folder is closed, the circle can be rotated so only one paired question and answer appears in the windows at a time. Directions for making a Disc-a-Test and four other self-testing devices may be found in Better Media Volume Two (see Bibliography).
2. An electric response board is a piece of heavy cardboard, masonite board, or wood large enough to hold a transparent plastic pocket for a sheet of 8½" x 11" paper. The paper contains a matching exercise, with a list of questions on the left side and a list of answers (in scrambled order) on the right side. There is a metal contact point for each question and answer. The board is wired so that when students make direct contact between a question and its answer with a probe, a light shows either on the board or on the probe. Directions for making several versions of this board may be found in Classroom Learning Centers (see Bibliography).

CHECKERS

The game of Checkers may be adapted for use as a review game.

Here's How:

1. Obtain a checkerboard with twelve black and twelve red checkers. Put a piece of masking tape or a gummed round label on each checker so the checkers can be numbered from one to twelve in both colors. Place them in

position on the board as for a regular game.

2. Type a list of twenty-four questions and answers based on the story, numbering each to correspond to a checker on the board (e.g., Black-1, Red-10, etc.). Since the questions probably will not be dealt with in sequence, they should be independent of one another.

3. Give these directions: Play the game according to the regular rules for Checkers, <u>except</u> that players cannot jump their opponents' checkers until they can correctly answer the questions corresponding to the numbers on the checkers to be jumped. If they cannot answer the questions correctly, they cannot complete their moves and their opponents take over. The player with the most checkers at the end of the game is the winner. A teacher or student reads the questions and determines whether the answers given are correct.

FISH BOWL GAME

Questions and answers in this self-testing review game can be used after students have heard a Bible story.

Here's How:

1. Prepare a fishing license to give students when they have finished listening to and discussing a Bible story. The license should grant them permission to fish for questions and answers in the Fish Bowl.

2. Cut out fish for the game from folded construction paper in a variety of bright colors, using the pattern below. Add eyes and other lines with a black marking pen.

3. Make a list of ten to fifteen short questions, one for each fish. Type a question on the outside of each fish, and type the answer on the inside so it is hidden when the fish is folded. Fasten a paper clip to the mouth of each fish so it can be caught

with a fishing pole made by tying one end of a piece of string to a pierced kitchen magnet and the other end to a dowel stick about 12 inches long. Place the fish in a glass fish bowl.

4. Give these directions: Two or three students may go fishing at one time. They take turns trying to catch the fish. The student who catches a fish tries to answer the question written on it. If successful (the answer written inside the fish serves as a checkpoint), the fish is kept. If the student's answer was wrong, the fish must be thrown back in the bowl. Play continues until all the fish have been caught and kept. The player with the most fish at the end of the game is the winner.

HOPSCOTCH

The children's game of Hopscotch, usually played on a sidewalk outdoors, can be used as the basis for an indoors review game.

Here's How:

1. Use masking tape to mark out a Hopscotch diagram on the floor of your classroom area. Mark the squares with numbered 3" x 5" cards taped in place (see below).

2. Provide red and black checkers for the players to use as markers and a beanbag for choosing a square.

3. Make a list of ten questions based on a Bible story. Number them to

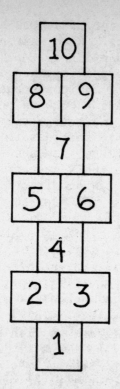

BIBLE BASEBALL

A question and answer game using the format of a baseball game can help students recall facts about characters or events in a Bible story or a story's cultural and historical background.

Here's How:

1. Locate three bases and home plate in your classroom area. Mark with signs.
2. Prepare the "balls," or questions, that you will throw to the batters as the pitcher. On individual cards, write short questions about the story, using letters large enough to be seen from the batter's box. Write the answers to the questions on the opposite sides of the cards.
3. Divide the students into two teams.
4. Give these instructions: The teams take turns being at bat, with the teacher serving as a stationary pitcher. The pitcher holds up questions for the batters in turn. If the batters answer their questions correctly, they move to first base, and any base runners ahead of them move on accordingly. If they give incorrect answers, they are out. When one team has three outs, the other team is up. Play continues so long as time permits or until all the balls have been thrown. Runners who reach home plate score one point for their team. The team with the most points at the end of the game is the winner.

BOARD GAMES

When you want to use a board game to help students remember a Bible story, develop one yourself instead of trying to find one that is commercially produced. That way you can guarantee that the game's approach to the story will be consistent with the way you

correlate with the squares on the diagram. Since the questions will not be dealt with in sequence, they should be independent of one another.
4. Give these directions: Two students may play this game. One uses red checkers and the other black checkers to mark their squares. Players take turns hopping in all the squares to ten, facing away from the diagram, and tossing the beanbag over their shoulders to get it on a square. They have three tries to get the beanbag on a square. If unsuccessful, they lose their turn. If successful, they have a chance to answer the question for that square. A right answer enables them to put their checker on that square. A wrong answer means the square is still available for both players. Once squares are claimed, players can hop on their own but must not hop on those of their opponents. If they do, they lose their turn. Play continues until all the squares have been claimed. The player with the most squares wins.

have used it in your sessions with the students.

Here's How:

1. Choose a Bible story that has a strong plot with plenty of action, such as the story of Jonah. Rewrite the story in short sentences, numbering each in sequence so they can easily be transferred to the board. For example:

    1. God calls Jonah to preach to Nineveh.
    2. Jonah doesn't want to help his enemies.

2. Board games usually introduce the element of chance, not only in the procedure used to move players around the board, but also in the way certain moves direct players to wait a turn or move backwards or forwards a given number of spaces. Consider your story again, and look for logical points to introduce this element of chance. For example:

--Jonah decides to run away. Wait one turn while he packs his bag.
--Jonah goes to Joppa. Wait one turn while he buys a ticket.
--Jonah spends three days and nights in the fish. Wait with him for three turns.
--The fish spits out Jonah onto dry land. Go back to Start.
--This time Jonah obeys God's call. Move ahead three spaces.

3. Look for places in the story where you can add other activities for humor and interest. For example:

--Jonah goes to sleep below the deck. Sing a lullabye to him ("Good Night, Jonah" to the tune of "Good Night, Ladies").
--The sailors cast lots to see who has caused the storm by angering the gods. Draw straws with the other players. The one with the short straw moves ahead three spaces.

--Jonah is angry that God has forgiven his enemies. Read what he says to God in Jonah 4:1-2.

4. Draw a course for the game on a piece of 22" x 28" posterboard, first with pencil and then with permanent marking pens in several colors. Divide the course into sections to correspond with the number of sentences in your story. Write the sentences within each section. When directions for game moves are too long to fit in the sections, write them on cards for a draw pile and direct the players to choose them in sequence or by number. Illustrate the game board with pictures from the story, drawn free-hand or copied from book illustrations.

5. Devise counters to use in the game. For example, counters for a game based on Jonah could be sailboats made by fastening colorful construction paper sails to Toggle Toy blocks with toothpick masts. Squares of posterboard, illustrated with symbols related to the story, may also be used.

6. Decide on what procedure to use in moving the players around the board: One die, two dice, a coin (one space for heads, two spaces for tails,) a spinner from another game, or others.

7. Make up a directions card by typing the rules for the game on paper and mounting it on posterboard with rubber cement. Include how many persons may play the game, how they determine their moves, and how the game is won. You may also want to raise a question about the story for the students to discuss when they have finished playing the game.

SEE ALSO:
 Bingo
 Password

Want to Know More?

Students need to know how to find out more about the cultural and historical background of a story through research in various reference books. What else was happening in the world when the story occurred? Who wrote the story and when? What meaning did it have for the people for whom it was written?

WRITING AS ANOTHER PERSON

When students are asked to assume the role of a biblical character in order to write as that character, they are motivated to do some research about the times and situations in which the person lived. The writing can take the form of a diary or a letter.

Here's How:

1. In a diary, the student selects one or more important events in the life of a biblical person and writes about them as if he or she were that person.
2. In a letter, the student describes important events to family members or friends (real or imaginary) and tells how the events have affected his or her life and feelings.

Try This:
The letter-writing technique would be useful in a study of Paul, since the apostle wrote many letters to the new churches he founded. The students could be given the name of one of these churches and a description of its problems (e.g., the argument over whether a new Christian had to follow the Jewish laws) and asked to write a letter to them as if they were Paul. They would be given a list of biblical references to consult so they could use the format of Paul's letters in the greeting and closing and could include the decision of the council of leaders in Jerusalem in Paul's advice.

INTERVIEWS

The opportunity to impersonate a biblical character in a taped interview will encourage students to do some research on that character, especially if they are guided by a list of questions that the interviewer will ask.

Here's How:

1. Choose an important character from a Bible story, such as Peter.

2. Make out a list of questions to be asked in the interview, citing references. For example:

Where are you from, Peter? (Matthew 8: 5, 14)

What is your occupation? (Matthew 4: 18)

How well did you know Jesus? (Matthew 10:1-4)

How did you feel about him? (Matthew 14:22-33; 16:13-20; 26:30-35)

What did you and the other disciples do after Jesus was crucified? (John 20:19)

What did Jesus ask you and the other disciples to do when he appeared to you after the Resurrection? (Luke 24:45-49)

How did the Resurrection change your lives? What did you do once you knew Jesus had overcome death? (see People of the Bible, pp. 124-27.)

3. Suggest that the students look up the references for each question and use them in preparing their answers for the interview. Have a member of the teaching team ready to conduct the interview, recording it live on a cassette recorder. (If students are to act as the interviewers, they should also do the research so they will be able to ask additional questions, as necessary, to help those taking the part of Peter round out an incomplete answer or to deal with an incorrect reply.)

4. Record the interview in a recording studio set up in a corner of the classroom. Don't worry about background noise. It will add realism to your on-the-spot interviews! Share the tapes later with others in the class.

WRITING A NEWSPAPER

How would today's newspaper read if it had been published in some period of Bible times? Making up such a newspaper involves students in a variety of research and creative writing activities.

Here's How:

1. Have students look at several newspapers and list the different kinds of materials in it. For example: editorials, lead news articles, advertisements, cartoons and comics, sports, letters to the editor, society news, featured stories and interviews, advice column, weather, and obituaries.

2. Decide together what kinds of things will be in your newspaper. Make assignments, taking the students' preferences into consideration.

3. Provide a variety of resources for research: Bible reference books, curriculum pieces, magazines, mounted pictures, audio-visuals, and others.

4. When the students have finished their research and writing or drawing assignments, have them make a mock-up of the newspaper by gluing their materials to a sheet of blank newsprint.

5. When the students are satisfied with the newspaper, have it typed and mimeographed so it can be shared with the congregation.

Try This:

Newspapers could be published for these biblical story-events: the Exodus, David, Amos, Jeremiah, Elijah, Holy Week, Pentecost, and Paul's visits to Jerusalem.

TAPING A NEWSCAST

If there had been radio or television in Bible times, what would a newscast have been like? Planning and taping a simulated newscast based on the events in a Bible story will appeal to students who enjoy working with a tape recorder more than working with a pen.

Here's How:

1. Help the students analyze the contents of radio and television

newscasts by listening to some together. (Tape them ahead of time to use in class.)

2. Decide what items you will include in the newscast (e.g., lead news articles, interviews, editorials, sports and society news, weather, advertisements, recipes, international news, and others).

3. Assign responsibilities for planning each item.

4. Provide a variety of resources for student research.

5. After the students have written out or shared verbally their contributions to the newscast and you have helped them with the editing, have them record the newscast on tape. Share it later with parents or the congregation, or use it as a resource in other classes.

PAPER BAG SURPRISE

Assignments for student research can be combined with mystery, neighborliness, and even refreshments!

Here's How:

1. For each student, prepare a paper bag with the instructions for the session's tasks written on individual slips of paper. The contents should be identical for each student's bag. For example:
--Eat a cookie.
--Choose a picture on the table that reminds you of Jesus, and put it in your bag until sharing time.
--Tell someone on your left, "Have a good day."
--Have a drink of punch.
--Read Mark 8:27-33 in your Bible.
--Look up "Messiah" in the Bible dictionary.
--Find someone across the room and ask him or her to tell you something good that happened this week.
--Gather with the other students for sharing at ____(state specific time.)

--Look at the rebus poster puzzles for the twelve disciples. Each one is numbered. Match the number of each puzzle correctly with the names of the disciples listed below. (Include the list of names.)

2. Prepare your classroom area for the activities you have selected. For example:
--A table with mounted magazine pictures chosen at random (e.g., a child holding a father's hand might remind students that Jesus trusted God)
--A refreshment table with punch, cups, cookies, and napkins
--A table with several Bible dictionaries and Bibles on it
--A display of rebus poster puzzles for the twelve disciples

3. Give these directions: The students pull out the slips of paper, one at a time, in any order, and follow the instructions on each. If they pull out one that has a time written on it, and it is not yet that time, they put it back and take another instead. They follow each instruction only once.

4. When the students gather together at the appointed time, have them share and discuss the results of their research. For example:
--Have the students show their pictures and tell why they chose them.
--Explain that the people in Jesus' day had to decide what they thought of Jesus. Some, like the disciples, chose to follow him. Check the answers to rebus poster puzzles, and then ask the students why they think these men became disciples.
--Ask for a report on "Messiah."
--Read Mark 8:27-33 as students follow in their Bibles.
--Note that Jesus wondered what people thought of him, and finally asked the disciples what they believed.
--Explain that Jesus' ideas of his mission was to be God's servant,

not a king or soldier. Reread
Mark 8:31.
--Suggest that Jesus may have gotten
this idea from the prophecy of
Isaiah. Read Isaiah 53:1-9, explaining that though the prophet
was thinking of the Jewish people
as God's servant, the idea fits
Jesus too.

CLASSROOM DICTIONARY

When students are confronted with a
number of new words in a story, it is
wise to plan a learning activity
around vocabulary research.

Here's How:

1. Post a ruled newsprint chart on
the bulletin board. Write "Classroom
Dictionary" at the top. On separate
pieces of lightweight cardboard, print
the key words from the story, one word
per card. Provide Bible dictionaries,
marking pens, and T-pins or tacks.
Explain to the students that they may
choose a word, post it on the chart,
look it up in the dictionary, and
write its definition on the chart.
2. Instead of a chart, have the
students write the words and definitions on relevant shapes (e.g.,
footprints for a story about Paul
who walked a lot in his work) cut
from brightly colored construction
paper or posterboard. Post these
somewhere in the room as they are

finished (e.g., footprints could
indicate a road across the walls
and ceiling.)

WORKSHEETS

Teacher-prepared worksheets can lead
students to Bible reference books to
find information about people, dates,
terms, and events in a Bible story.

Here's How:

1. Design a worksheet with two
columns. In the left column, write
passages from the Bible story, underlining new words or phrases and references to people, places, or times
that are important to understanding
the story. Opposite each passage, in
the right column, ask a question about
the words you have underlined, leaving
space for the students to write in an
answer.
2. Mimeograph copies of the worksheet
for each student. Provide reference
books for their research.

SEE ALSO:
  Guided Bible Study
  Time Lines
  Model Scenes
  Wall Maps
  Overhead Transparency Maps
  Word Search Puzzle
  Crossword Puzzle Variations
  Bingo
  Use of Concordance

How Is It Spelled?

Students need to know how to spell terms, concepts, and the names of characters and places in a story correctly in order to work with it intelligibly. Will others know what they mean when they write these words?

SCRAMBLED WORDS

If students can unscramble a word and put the letters in proper order, they know how to spell it.

Here's How:

1. Select key words from a story. They may be names of persons or places or important terms. Scramble up the letters in each. Ask the students to rearrange the letters so each word is spelled correctly.
2. If desired, combine this activity with another exercise. For example, after unscrambling the words the students may use them to match with given definitions or complete a crossword puzzle.

ALPHABET CARDS FOR NAMES OR TERMS

Individual cards for all the letters in each name or term important to a Bible story can be used in several ways.

Here's How:

1. Divide the students into two teams. Mix up all the letters from all the words and lay them on a table. At a given signal, the students try to form words from the individual letters and pin them on the bulletin board as they succeed. The team with the most correct answers wins. For example, students were asked to sort out letters to form the names of the twelve disciples of Jesus. They soon discovered that they didn't know who these men were. Looking up "disciple" in a Bible dictionary sent them to a Bible reference where the twelve were listed. As they returned to their spelling task, they began to realize that they had to work together as teams, and sometimes they had to trade letters with the other team in order to spell the words correctly. The exercise had the dual purpose of a spelling drill and an exercise in learning how to work together as the disciples must have had to do.
2. Give the students envelopes containing letters for one name or term. Direct them to assemble the letters to spell a word that means --------(here give a definition) or a name for the person who --------(here give an identi-

fication). Ask them to use the reference books available to see what else they can learn about the term or biblical character.

HIDDEN PEOPLE

All the letters in the names of key persons in a story can be scattered at random on a page for the students to form into words.

Here's How:

1. Write the letters from the names you have chosen at random on a worksheet. If a letter is used more than once, it should be repeated as many times as it appears. For example, names from the Exodus story could be written as follows:

Provide lines at the bottom of the worksheet where students can write down the names as they spell them.
2. Give these directions: Find the names of six people from the story of the Exodus in these letters, and write them correctly below. Use each letter only once in a name. (Answers: Moses, Aaron, Miriam, Joshua, Jethro, Zipporah. Have these in an envelope for checking answers.)

WORDS ARE HIDING

The letters of two related words can be mixed together for the students to unscramble and spell correctly.

Here's How:

1. Make a list of pairs of words that have a common meaning. (At least one

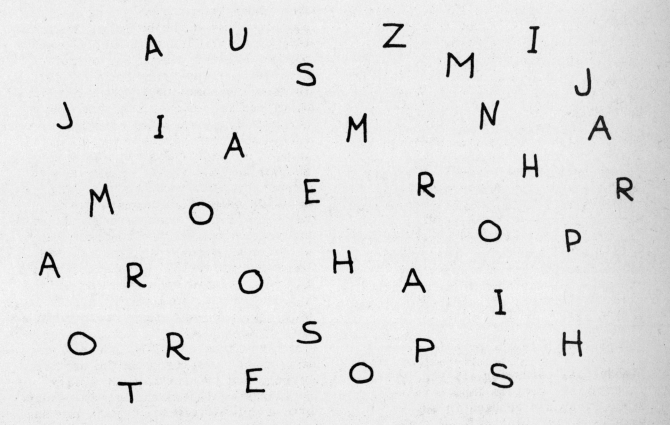

53

of the words should be from the story the students are learning.)

2. Mix up the letters in each pair, but keep them in the order in which they appear in each word. Give the common definition as a clue. For example:

APRGROEMEMISENET Two words
that mean covenant
(agreement, promise)

BFAELIETHF Two words
that mean trust
(belief, faith)

HORNESOPECRT Two words
that mean worship
(honor, respect)

Try This:
Pairs of related names could also be used for this exercise. Check the Index for "Who Are We? A Game of Pairs."

WORD GAME

Spelling new words is easier when you don't have to write them down. This game involves manipulating Scrabble-like letters to spell words.

Here's How:

1. Make a list of key words from a Bible story. They may be names of persons or places or terms.

2. Cut posterboard pieces in two sizes: squares the size of Scrabble game letters and larger squares or oblongs with room for a word.

3. Write a letter of the alphabet on each small square, being sure to include an ample supply of each letter in proportion to its use in the words selected for the game. On each of the larger cards, write one of the words you have chosen.

4. On the bulletin board near the game table, post a chart of the words used in the game with their definitions.

5. Give these directions: Two to four children or pairs of children may play. Place the alphabet cards face up on

the center of the table, with the word cards face down in a pile beside them. The first player turns up a word card so all can see it. The players quickly try to build the word with the alphabet cards. The first player to complete the word wins one point. A correct definition of the word will earn the player a second point. The first player to earn five points wins the game.

SPELLING RELAY

Spelling key words from a story can be the basis for a relay.

Here's How:

1. Make a list of words from the story which the students should be learning to spell.

2. On 3" x 5" cards, using one letter per card, write the letters that occur in the words, repeating those that appear more than once in any given word. Make a set of these cards for each team.

3. Make a list of questions, each of which may be answered by one of the above words.

4. Divide the students into two or more teams, and give each one a set of letter cards. Position each team an equal distance from a central table.

5. Give these directions: The teams distribute the letter cards in their set among their members so each has at least one card. The teacher asks a question that may be answered by a word spelled out with some of the letter cards. The members on each team decide on an answer, select the letter cards needed, run to the table, and lay out their cards to spell the word. The first team to lay out the correct word scores a point. Play continues until all the questions have been answered. The team with the most points wins.

COMMERCIALLY PRODUCED GAMES

It is possible to use a game like Probe, manufactured by Parker Brothers, as a spelling exercise for words from a Bible story. The game involves two, three, or four players at a time in selecting words of twelve letters or less and spelling them out with cards hidden from the other players' eyes. Players take turns trying to guess the letters in one another's words, so they can discover the words themselves.

Here's How:

1. Make a list of words from the story that have twelve letters or less. Post the words near the game table, and suggest that the students choose words from this list for the game.
2. Play according to the rules, except award an extra point to the player who can identify or define the word discovered.

Try This:
Before you go out to buy the game, ask families in your congregation if they have one to lend.

SEE ALSO:
Word Search Puzzle
Crossword Puzzles and Variations

What Do the Words Mean?

Students need to be able to define the meanings of key concepts and ideas and new terms used in the stories. When they use the word "covenant," are they all talking about the same thing?

GO FISH

A popular children's card game may be used as the format for developing a game based on key concepts from a story and their definitions.

Here's How:

1. Select six key concepts from a story. For each concept, make a list of four brief definitions, synonyms, or examples. For example, if you are dealing with the story of David you might list:

Chosen
1. anointed
2. picked by God
3. given a job to do
4. David

Sin
1. breaking the covenant
2. disobeying God
3. selfishness
4. stealing another man's wife

Prophet
1. speaks for God
2. tells God's plan for people
3. tries to get people to follow God's plan
4. Nathan

Covenant
1. an agreement between two parties
2. a contract
3. a promise to be loyal to one another
4. relationship between God and the Hebrew people.

Trust
1. faith
2. depending on someone
3. counting on a friend to help you
4. believing God will forgive you

King
1. chosen by God to rule
2. responsible to God
3. Saul
4. David

2. Use commercially produced blank playing cards (see Bibliography) to make four cards for each concept. At the top of each card write the concept in large letters. Below, write one of the definitions or examples you have listed. Number the cards for each concept in order from one to four.

3. Give these directions: Two to four persons may play at a time. Deal three cards to each player. Lay the additional cards face down on the table. The object of the game is for each player to make as many books (all four cards for a concept) as possible. Players take turns asking one another for concept cards to match those in their hands. For example, one player might ask another, "Do you have any King cards?" That player would have to give up any King cards held or if blank in that concept, would say, "Go fish." The first player would then draw a card from those on the table, keeping it without discarding another. The second player would now have a chance to ask someone for concept cards. Play continues until all the cards on the table have been drawn. (If there are still cards on the table when some players hold complete books in their hands, they would simply draw a card from the table and ask for more cards for that concept when it is their turn.) The player with the most books wins the game.

SCRAMBLED WORDS AND DEFINITIONS

Matching words correctly with their definitions is an exercise that may be used in several settings. Students in a learning center could work with a set of word cards and definition cards individually or in competition with one another. A larger set of cards, with words visible from a distance, could be unscrambled by students, arranged on a bulletin board, and left as a display during the unit.

Here's How:

1. Make a list of new words from a story and their definitions.
2. Decide how you will use the exercise. This will determine the size of the cards you buy. The cards should be in two colors, one for words and the other for definitions.

3. On cards of one color, write the words, one word per card. On cards of the other color, write the definitions, one per card.
4. Ask the students to match the words correctly with the definitions.

SCRAMBLED SENTENCE DEFINITIONS FOR THE FELT BOARD

The words within a sentence definition for a key concept or a word in a story may be scrambled up for students to rearrange correctly on a felt board.

Here's How:

1. Use brightly colored marking pens to write each word in a sentence definition on a separate piece of light-weight cardboard or paper. Glue felt or nonwoven interfacing on the back of each word. Mix them up.
2. Provide a flannelboard or felt board (described in Better Media for Less Money, p. 24) for the students to use and an answer key with the correct definition.
3. Give these directions: Arrange the words on the felt board so they correctly define _____.
When you have finished, check your sentence with the key. Correct any mistakes that you have made, and then mix up the words for the next student to use.

DEFINITIONS RELAY

Matching terms and definitions can be used as the basis for a relay.

Here's How:

1. Make a list of terms from your story and their definitions. For example, you might use the following from a story about how Jesus taught his disciples to pray:

Term	Definition
Name	The title by which a person is known
Kingdom	The rule of God
Trespasses	Wrongdoing
Father	Name used by Jesus for God to help people know what God was like
Hallowed	Holy; set apart; treated with reverence
Evil	Opposite of good
Forgive	To pardon someone who has done wrong
Our daily bread	All the things we need to live
Will	That which a person wants to happen
Temptation	Being tested

2. Write each definition on a separate card. Make one set of these cards for each team.

3. Give these directions: Divide the group into two or more teams. Each team should have a set of definition cards. After the teacher reads a term, the members of each team decide together on the correct definition for the term. Then they send a runner up to the teacher with the definition card they have selected. The first runner to deliver a correct answer scores one point. The team with the most points at the end of the relay wins.

FLASHCARDS

Flashcards with pictures, as well as words, can help nonreaders and beginning readers learn to define new words from a story.

Here's How:

1. Read through the story carefully, making a list of key words that are new to the students. Consider how the definitions for these words could be illustrated with simple stick-figure or line drawings, or pictures cut from curriculum resources.

2. Make flashcards from 5½" x 14" pieces of posterboard. On one side, print the word in large letters. On the other side, illustrate the definition for the word. For example, you might make flashcards for the story of how David soothed King Saul with his music as follows:

Shepherd -- man taking care of sheep on a hillside

King -- man with a crown, seated and surrounded by people on a lower level

Lyre -- a stringed instrument

Soldier -- a man dressed in armor, carrying weapons

Armor-bearer -- boy carrying armor and weapons

3. Use the flashcards to introduce new words and their meanings.

KEY WORD ANALYSIS

Helping students focus on a few selected words or phrases in a Bible story can give them the key to understanding the passage better.

Here's How:

1. Ask the students to read through the story, jotting down the words or phrases that they feel are most important. For example, in Acts 3:1-10, the key words might be: Peter, John, lame man, alms, look, expecting, receive, in the name of Jesus Christ, walk, raise, leaping, walked, praising God, wonder, amazement.

2. Have them report their findings as you list the key words on newsprint, a blackboard, or the overhead projector.

3. Help the students play around with the words: Which are emotion words? Which words involve action? Which words deal with persons? Try adding some of your own words to the key words to make a short, complete account of the story.

SIMULATED EXPERIENCES, USING COMMERCIALLY PRODUCED GAMES

Sometimes commercially produced games can be used to set up simulated experiences to help students define a concept.

Here's How:

1. Assemble enough construction-type toys such as Tinker Toys, Lego Blocks, an erector set, or others, so all the students will have some materials to use. Explain to the students that they may choose one of the construction toys and make something with it, working alone or with others. They will have twenty minutes in which to work. At the end of this time, ask the students to share any problems they have encountered: For example, deciding on a design, changing their minds about a design after starting on it, running out of time or materials, or lacking the skill to build their design. Then raise this question: Does God have any of these problems in creating our world? Why, or why not? Help the students discover through discussion that God's creative powers are not limited by time, space, materials, power, skill, or plan.

2. Use the Monopoly game manufactured by Parker Brothers. Have one game for every four to six students. Before the students arrive, lay out the game board, cards, counters, dice, and money. Deal out the money in unequal portions so several of the players start the game at a disadvantage. Explain to the students that you have done this to save time. Tell them that they will be able to play for a specified length of time (40-45 minutes), and then the player with the most money and property will be declared the winner. At the end of the game, be sure to praise and honor the winner. Then confess that the winner has won because he or she had been dealt the most money. Accept the students' feelings and relate them through discussion to the concepts of "justice" and "injustice."

PASSWORD

The Password game made popular by television and the play-at-home version manufactured by Milton Bradley Company can serve as the model for a classroom contest designed to help students learn the definitions of important words from a story.

Here's How:

1. Make a list of concepts and terms from a story or group of stories. For example, from the story of the Exodus you might select: commandments, exodus, sin, covenant, sabbath, Passover, Yahweh, idol, manna, plague, Pharaoh, slave.

2. Make two cards for each concept or term.

3. Give these directions: Divide the students into two teams. Each team chooses one member to receive the first word from the leader. The leader gives the cards for a concept or term to each team representative. They take turns giving one-word clues to their respective teams who try to guess the word from the clues. Members of a team may work together, but only one person may give an answer from each team. (The teams alternate in giving the first clue.)

4. Scoring is as follows: If a team guesses right on the first clue, it scores ten points; on the second clue, nine; third clue, eight; fourth clue, seven; fifth clue, six; and sixth clue, five. If after a total of six clues have been given (three by each team representative) the word has not been guessed, the leader gives the correct answer and no points are given. The teams then choose other representatives to give the next clue, and

59

play resumes with a new word. The team with the highest score at the end of the game wins.

BINGO

Students enjoy testing their knowledge of terms and definitions in a game patterned after the game of Bingo manufactured by Whitman Company. The games can be designed by either the teachers or the students.

Here's How:

1. Make a list of thirty to thirty-five different terms from a story or group of stories, with their definitions.
2. Use 7½-inch square pieces of posterboard for the game cards. Rule each card off into 1¼-inch squares so there are twenty-five squares on every card. An easy way to do this is to use one card as a pattern. Cut notches at 1¼-inch intervals on all sides. Lay the pattern on the 7½-inch square, and mark the card at the notches with a pencil. Remove the pattern, and use a ruler and permanent marking pen to draw in the lines, using the notches as guides. Label the center square on each card "free." On each of the other squares, write a term from your list, varying the arrangement so that each card is different.
3. Make cards for the caller from posterboard cut in 2 3/4-inch squares. On each one, write a definition for one of the terms on your list.
4. For counters, use old buttons, small posterboard squares, dried corn, or counters from a commercially produced Bingo game.
5. Give these directions: Each person selects a game card and puts a counter on the free square. The caller draws a card and reads the definition on it. Players who think they have the corresponding term on their cards place a counter on that square. Play continues until one player has five

squares covered in a row across, down, or diagonally, and calls "Bingo!" The caller checks to see that the answers are correct. If so, the players clear their cards and start a new game. Black-out (in which all the squares must be covered) or Four Corners (the squares on each corner must be covered) versions of the game may also be played.

PICTURE LOTTO

Illustrations from a Bible story may be used to construct a Picture Lotto game that will help students identify key concepts or characters from the story.

Here's How:

1. Choose a theme. For example, you might develop a game around the concepts of Jesus as teacher, preacher, healer, forgiver of sins, Messiah, and risen Lord.
2. Collect pictures illustrating Jesus in these different roles from old curriculum pieces, greeting cards, church bulletins, magazines, calendars, church supply catalogs, and other sources. You will need two copies of each picture. Sort the pictures so you have two identical groups for each role.
3. Use 14" x 22" pieces of posterboard for the Lotto cards, making one card for each role. Glue one set of each group of pictures on this backing with rubber cement, according to the method described in Better Media for Less Money, pp. 27-28 (see Bibliography). Write a title (for example, "Jesus, the Teacher") on each card. Cover the cards with transparent, self-adhesive vinyl to protect them from handling.
4. Use the duplicate sets of pictures to make the game pieces. Cut each picture down so only a part of it is shown. Mount each picture and cover as above. On the reverse side of each

picture, write a brief description of the event it illustrates. For example, on the back of a picture showing Jesus as a preacher, write: "Jesus preached to the people, 'Repent, for the kingdom of heaven is at hand.'" Put these game pieces in a box or large envelope, with the following instructions written on the outside:

How to Play: Six people may play at a time. If there are fewer than six, divide the extra cards among the players. Players take turns drawing game pieces, one at a time. If the pieces match pictures on their Lotto cards, they place them on their cards. If they do not match, the players replace the pieces in the box or envelope. The person who first matches game pieces to all the pictures on a Lotto card wins. Before the cards are cleared for another game, the winner reads what is written on the back of each game piece on the winning card. If they prefer, players may continue playing until all the game pieces are matched with the Lotto cards correctly before starting a new game.

Try This:
1. Make a Picture Lotto game based on key figures from the Old Testament (e.g., Abraham, Jacob, Joseph, Moses, David, some of the prophets), and use it as the basis for review of a group of Bible stories.
2. Use duplicate magazine pictures as the basis for a Picture Lotto game on key concepts common to many Bible stories (e.g., covenant, trust, love, worship).

CONCEPT MOBILES

Pictures can help students discover the meaning of concepts or key words from a story.

Here's How:

1. Choose one or more concepts or key words from a story.
2. For each concept or word, collect a group of pictures to illustrate its meaning. The pictures may be from magazines, curriculum resources, calendars, Sunday bulletin covers, and other sources. For example, when dealing with the story of Amos, the concept of injustice could be illustrated with pictures of poverty, starvation, discrimination, conspicuous consumption, entertainment stars, and sports figures. News headlines could also be included.
3. Mount the pictures in each group on both sides of pieces of lightweight cardboard, one picture per side. Punch a hole in the top of each picture so wire or string can be inserted and used to suspend each picture from a coathanger or piece of wooden dowel for a mobile. Add a sign: "What idea is common to all the pictures?"
4. Use the mobile as a starter for group discussion on the concept.

Try This:
Instead of a mobile, mount the pictures for one concept or word on the four sides of several medium-sized cardboard cartons. Stack them vertically to form a kiosk. Post the same sign.

MONTAGE

A montage is a composite picture made by combining several pictures in an attractive arrangement on a background to illustrate a common theme or concept. It is a way to focus attention on the meaning of a concept for the purpose of discussion or worship.

Here's How:

1. Use a piece of posterboard or cardboard cut from a carton as the backing.
2. Select a group of pictures to illustrate a concept from a story. For example, for the story of the Exodus you could use pictures like these to illustrate the concept of laws: a stop sign, a sign reading Please Keep Off the Grass, stone tablets bearing the Ten Commandments (or Roman numerals from one to ten,) a judge in a courtroom, children washing their hands before eating, a Bible opened to Exodus 20, and so forth.
3. Mount the pictures on the backing, using the dry rubber cement method described in Better Media for Less Money, beginning on p. 27 (see Bibliography). Arrange the pictures so that no matter how the backing is turned, at least one picture will appear right side up.

MONTAGE JIGSAW PUZZLES

A montage picture illustrating a concept or key word may be cut apart for use as a jigsaw puzzle.

Here's How:

1. Use lightweight cardboard, brown paper grocery bags, or construction paper for the backing. Cut apart, as for a jigsaw puzzle. Provide a magnetic board (a metal door or filing cabinet, a child's magnetic alphabet board, or a magnetic white board) and kitchen magnets for the students to use in assembling the puzzle. Challenge them to discover what concept the puzzle illustrates.
2. Use lightweight cardboard for the backing, and then glue on felt or nonwoven interfacing on the back of

that. Cut the montage apart, as for a jigsaw puzzle, and provide a felt board (see Better Media for Less Money, p. 24) for the students to use in assembling it.

PICK-A-PICTURE BOX

An ordinary cardboard carton, decorated and labeled "Pick-a-Picture Box," may be filled with mounted pictures illustrating a concept or key word from a story. The pictures can be used in several ways to stimulate discussion on the concept.

Here's How:

1. Fill the box with mounted pictures of everyday life situations that illustrate a concept. For example, trust is involved when a boy flies a kite, a logger fells a tree, a child jumps into a father's arms, a baby holds a parent's hand while learning to walk, a cook follows a recipe, an air traffic controller guides a plane to the runway, a parachutist jumps, a doctor examines a child, a couple is married. Divide the students into small groups. Ask each group to choose a picture and use it as the basis of a skit that uses the word "trust." (Be sure to have more pictures than groups, so each group will have a choice.) After the skits have been shared the students can work on a common definition of trust.
2. Use pictures of something that is used symbolically in the concept but is familiar to the students for other reasons. For example, when dealing with the story of Jesus' baptism, you could use pictures of water in various forms: rain on a growing field, a bubbly bathtub, a child in a shower, a geyser, a waterfall, a clear mountain river or lake, a drinking fountain, children in raincoats playing in a mud puddle. Ask the students to look through the pictures so each one can select one that shows what water does for us. Have them share and explain

their choices. They may say water
makes us clean, helps things and people
grow, gives us power, gives us joy.
Then ask them why they think Christians
have used water in baptism. Help them
discover that baptism washes away the
badness of our lives, gives us a
chance for a new life and the power
to grow, and makes us full of joy in
God's love.

TELEGRAMS

Persons who send telegrams find it
necessary to write their messages as
concisely as possible because their
cost is determined at a fixed rate
per word. The telegram is a good
format to have students use when they
are studying a brief, but important,
passage of scripture and trying to
restate its central meaning in their
own words.

Here's How:

1. Choose a biblical passage, perhaps
from one of the prophets, from Paul's
letters, or from Jesus' teachings.
Discuss its meaning with the students,
and provide reference books to help
the students research its meaning.
Talk about the ideas in the passage
together.
2. Provide Western Union telegram
blanks or facsimiles. Explain to
the students that they are to pretend
they are the author of the biblical
passage they have been discussing
and want to express the ideas of the
passage in the telegram. Each word
costs 25¢ and they are allowed no
more than $2.50 each. Therefore,
they must write their messages as
concisely as possible.

WORD SEARCH PUZZLE

In this puzzle, words related to a
key concept are hidden among other
letters in the alphabet. The words
may read across, up, down, and
diagonally. For older students,
puzzles may be designed with some of
the words reading backwards. For
younger children, it may be helpful
to indicate each letter that starts
a new word by making it a different
color or underlining it.

Here's How:

1. Make a list of words related to
a key concept in a story. For example,
a key concept in the story of the
Exodus is "covenant." Words for the
puzzle might include: agreement,
contract, pledge, promise, pact, testament, bargain, bond, deal, compact.
2. Using graph paper, arrange the
words so that they intersect wherever
possible, reading across, up, down, or
diagonally. Fill in the empty squares
with letters of the alphabet chosen at
random. For example:

```
B A D U S O V W S T O X

U O R E B C N A M E P Q

P X N W A T I G R S A T

L R C D R N O R E T C H

E L O P G D N E S A T F

D D V M A G O E P M L O

G Z E R I U T M S E R Z

E L N A N S O E F N P T

H D A M L C E N W T K N

C O N T R A C T E J R S

F M T A U I R Z O R X H
```

3. Mimeograph copies of the puzzle to give to the students with these directions: Read the description of the relationship between God and the Israelites in Exodus 19:4-6a, 8. Find the word that describes this relationship in the puzzle, and draw a red circle around it. Use another color to circle the ten words in the puzzle that have the same meaning. Use one of these words to write a definition of the word you have circled in red.

CROSSWORD PUZZLES

Since commercially produced crossword puzzles based on the Bible usually cover too broad an area to be useful, it is better to develop original puzzles around words from a story or words related to key concepts in the story.

Here's How:

1. Make a list of the words you plan to use, checking carefully to see that each is spelled correctly. Use only words related to the story or its key concepts. Do not add words for filler. Class time is too precious to waste looking up irrelevant words.
2. Using graph paper, arrange the words so that they read across or down. It is easier if you start with the longest words. There must be an empty space between each word so the words do not run together, unless more than one word is used as the answer to a clue, and the clue so indicates.
3. Number the words consecutively every time a new word begins down or across, using the same number for down and across if the first letters starts both words; otherwise use a different number for each word.
4. Write out and number the clues for the words used across and down in proper order.
5. If you feel the students will need help in spelling the words in the

puzzle, list the words with the puzzle in scrambled order. Or scramble the letters in each word and list the words with the corresponding clue.
6. Make copies of the puzzle (leaving the squares for the letters blank) and clues for each student, adding these directions: Use the clues to help you find the words to complete the puzzle.

Try This:
1. Give students graph paper, a list of words, reference books to consult when writing clues, and the above instructions so they can make up their own puzzles.
2. Enlarge puzzles for use by a group of students instead of individuals. Outline the puzzle on the floor with masking tape. Write the clues on individual 3" x 5" cards and place them in a pile, face down. Make individual cards for each letter to be used in the puzzle, and lay them face up. Students can take turns drawing clues and using the letters to fill in the words. The same approach could be used with a puzzle outlined on a chalkboard with masking tape, except that the letters would be written in with chalk. Either puzzle could be cleared for use by another group of students after the first group had completed the puzzle.

CROSSWORD PUZZLE VARIATION 1

A crossword puzzle may be designed so that only the key concept reads across, and all the other words read down.

Here's How:

1. Choose a key concept and write it across the graph paper. For example, when students have been working with stories about Old Testament prophets, you might choose the concept "Messiah."
2. Fit in related terms in rows going

down, one word for each letter of the key concept. (The only across row that needs to form a word is the key concept.) For example, you might use words to indicate the kind of person the prophets thought the Messiah would be. Number the down words consecutively.

```
            1
            E
        2        5 6 7
        M S    4 K D C
            3
        M E S S I A H
        A R A H N V R
        N V V E G I I
        U A I P I D S
        E N O H D   T
        L T R E
              R
              D
```

3. Write out clues for the key concept and each of the terms. Use Bible reference books as a guide. For example:
1. His name will mean "God with us."
2. He will serve the people.
3. He will save the people from their enemies.
4. He will care for the people as a _____ who looks after the sheep.
5. He will rule the people on God's behalf.
6. He will be a descendant of this famous king.
7. He will be the "anointed one," chosen by God.

4. Make copies of the puzzle (omitting the letters for each word) for all the students, or make a large puzzle for the floor, chalkboard, or bulletin board. Include directions for the puzzle. For example: The missing words in the up-and-down columns describe the person the prophets thought God would send to help the Jews. Use the clues to help you fill in the letters for each one. When you have finished, a seven-letter word will

appear in one of the across rows. It is the title the Jews used for the one God had promised to send them. Draw a circle around that word.

CROSSWORD PUZZLE VARIATION 2

A crossword puzzle may be designed so that only the key concept reads down, and all the other words read across. Instead of a key concept, you might use a hidden message such as "Love your neighbor" from Jesus, or "Love one another" from Paul.

Here's How:

The procedure for designing this puzzle is the same as for Variation 1, except that the only up-and-down column that needs to form a word or words is the one with spaces for the key concept or hidden message. The numbered clues will correspond with the numbered rows across.

CROSSWORD PUZZLE VARIATION 3

A crossword puzzle may be designed with the key concept printed in the up-and-down column, and related words written in rows across. There should be one row across each letter in the key concept.

Here's How:

The procedure for designing this puzzle is the same as for the other variations, except that the key concept is printed in the puzzle to serve as an additional clue.

Try This:

```
      1 S P E A K S
      2 J E R E M I A H
      3 A M O S
      4 B A P T I S T
  5 I S A I A H
      6 E Z E K I E L
      7 N A T H A N
```

65

Clues:
1. A prophet _____ for God.
2. Prophet who talked about a new covenant based on love.
3. Prophet who was concerned about justice for the poor.
4. John the _____ was a prophet in the time of Jesus.
5. Prophet who spoke of the Suffering Servant whom God would send to save the people.
6. Prophet who saw strange visions and spoke of the Messiah as one who would care for his people like a shepherd.
7. Prophet who talked to King David about his sin.

A WORD PUZZLE IN RHYME

Rhyming clues help students discover each letter in a key concept or word from a story. Since the clues are written in the same sequence as the letters appearing in the word, their answers will spell the key concept vertically in the puzzle.

Here's How:

1. To design the puzzle, write a key concept or term from a story vertically on a piece of paper. Number each letter in sequence.
2. Opposite each letter in the word, write a clue, using this format: "My first is in _____ but not in ____." For the first blank, substitute a word containing the first letter of the concept; for the second blank, substitute a word without that letter. Continue in the same manner for the other clues.
3. Make copies of the puzzle for the students, leaving a blank for each of the letters in the key concept. Include these directions: Use the clues that are given to put one letter in the blank at the beginning of each line. The word that results was an important one for (character in the

story) or the word means (definition or synonym).

Try This:
1. _(T)_ My first is in faith, but not in fear;
2. _(R)_ The next in reliance, and also in cheer;
3. _(U)_ My third is in truth and justice as well;
4. _(S)_ My fourth in thanksgiving, but not in bell;
5. _(T)_ My fifth is in throne, but not in worry;
   Now solve the puzzle . . . do it in a hurry!

ACROSTICS

An acrostic is a word made up of the first letters of other words. Students can be challenged to make up acrostics for key concepts or terms from a story.

Here's How:

1. List several key concepts or terms that could be developed into acrostics. Let the students work with one of their own choice.
2. Have the students write the word they have chosen vertically on paper. Then ask them to write a word beginning with each letter of the vertical word across the page. The words should define or describe the concept or term. For example:

     L oyal
     O pen
     V aliant
     E nduring

(A thesaurus or dictionary will be helpful to the students for this project.)

SEE ALSO:
Comparison Cards
Experiments
Vicarious Experiences
Real Experiences
Simulated Experiences

Can You Repeat That?

Some parts of a story should be memorized for future use, but it doesn't have to be drudgery! Students can have fun memorizing parts of the Bible.

JIGSAW PUZZLE QUOTATIONS

Teachers may call attention to brief, but important biblical passages from a story by making them the basis for jigsaw puzzles.

Here's How:

1. Using a pencil, lightly sketch in jigsaw puzzle lines on a sheet of 8½" x 11" paper.
2. Write a biblical quotation on the paper, taking care that the puzzle lines do not separate the letters within a word.
3. Glue the paper to nonwoven interfacing, using the dry rubber cement method described in Better Media for Less Money, p. 24 (see Bibliography).
4. Cut the puzzle apart along the jigsaw puzzle lines, and store in an envelope labeled with the source of the quotation.
5. Provide a felt board for assembling the puzzle.

Try This:
1. After the students have assembled the quotation, have them use it as a reference for a related exercise. For example, in his letters, Paul often gave advice to the members of the churches he had founded about how to live as Christians. Some of this advice could be quoted on the jigsaw puzzles. The assembled puzzles could then be used by the students as a help in finding Paul's advice in a Word Search Puzzle, such as, Be kind, or Forgive.
2. The students can be asked to read the assembled quotation and show what it means to them by rewriting it in their own words.

NUMBER CODES

Key biblical passages from a story may be encoded for the students to decipher. A simple code can be developed by numbering the letters of the alphabet in consecutive order.

Here's How:

1. Write out the alphabet. Number each letter in consecutive order. For example:

```
A--1    G--7    M--13    T--20
B--2    H--8    N--14    U--21
C--3    I--9    O--15    V--22
D--4    J--10   P--16    W--23
E--5    K--11   Q--17    X--24
F--6    L--12   R--18    Y--25
                S--19    Z--26
```

2. Write out the biblical passage you have chosen, leaving space between each line so you can write the corresponding number above each letter. For example:

```
12 15 22 5   25 15 21 18
L  O  V  E   Y  O  U  R
```

```
14 5 9 7 8 2 15 18
N  E I G H B O  R
```

This is your answer key.

3. Prepare the passage in code for the students, leaving a blank for each letter below the corresponding number. Write in a few letters as a clue to the code. The passage will have to be long enough so the students will have enough clues to enable them to break the code.

ALPHABET SHIFT CODES

A code dating back to Roman emperors merely shifts the alphabet ahead or back a given number of letters. A simple decoder can be made to help encode and decode biblical passages in this way.

Here's How:

1. Type the alphabet in capital letters across a 4" x 6" card, leaving a space between each letter and a 3/4-inch margin on each side.

2. Below this row and outside each end, cut a vertical slit through which a strip of paper 3/4" x 11" can slide. Type the alphabet backwards from Z to A <u>twice</u> on the strip, with a space between each letter.

3. To use, choose a key letter and position it beneath the "A" on the card. Write out the biblical passage, using the letters on the strip that

appear under the desired letters on the card. Students can use the same decoder to decipher the passage if they are given the key letter. For example:

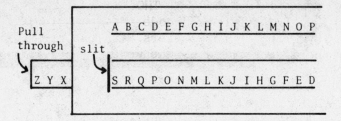

When "S" is the key letter, then "P" in the message would be written as "D," "H" in the message would be "L," and so on.

DUMMY LETTER CODES

Biblical passages may be encoded simply by adding the same or different "dummy" letters after every letter in the words of the passage.

Here's How:

1. Write out a biblical quotation, leaving a space after each letter. For example:
```
      G O D   I S   L O V E
```
2. Add the same or different "dummy" letters after each letter in the passage. For example:
```
   GWOWDW  IWSW  LWOWVWEW
or    GAOMDW  IZST  LAORVUEP
```
3. The passage may be decoded by copying down every other letter, starting with the first letter.

WORD SHIFT CODES

Words in a biblical quotation may be separated into different groupings for another code.

Here's How:

1. Write out a quotation. For example:

REMEMBER THE SABBATH DAY,
TO KEEP IT HOLY.

2. Separate the letters in the words in different ways to form new "words." For example:

RE MEMB ER THESA BBAT HDAY,
T OKE EPI THO LY.

3. The students decode the quotation by grouping the letters with the proper spaces between the words.

REVERSE CODES

The words of a biblical quotation may be written in reverse with the words run together as one word. To decipher it, the students must separate the words and write them in correct sequence. For example:

YLOHTIPEEKOT, YADHTABBASEHTREBMEMER

(Remember the Sabbath Day,
to keep it holy.)

RAIL-FENCE CODES

Short biblical quotations may be written in columns that are read from the top down in sequence from left to right. For example:

L V Y U N I H O
O E O R E G B R

To decipher the code, the students read the columns as directed and write the passage horizontally: Love your neighbor.

MAZE CODES

Short biblical quotations may be encoded in the form of a maze. To decipher these codes, students will need a key.

Here's How:

1. Count the number of letters in the quotation. Then mark off a square or oblong section of graph paper containing the corresponding number of squares.

2. Decide on the pattern for your maze code. It can read vertically, starting from any corner and moving up one column and down the next. Or it can read horizontally, starting from any corner and moving across one row and back the next. Make a key for the pattern you choose. For example:

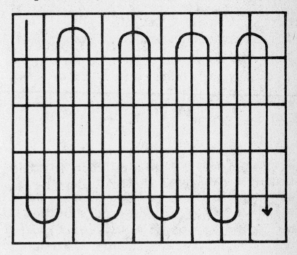

3. Write the quotation on the graph paper, following the pattern you have chosen. For example:

H	L	E	W	H	T	H	H	E
O	B	S	E	O	N	E	T	L
S	■	S	H	C	I	N	F	O
A	A	E	S	O	S	A	O	R
N	N	D	I	M	E	M	E	D

Mark 11:9

(If you have extra spaces, leave them blank between sentences or words.)

4. Duplicate the encoded quotation and the key for the students. Include the biblical reference also.

PIGPEN CODES

Biblical quotations may be written in a code that substitutes a symbol for each letter of the alphabet. Here is the code:

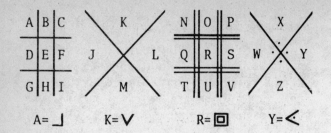

A= ⌐ K= V R= ⊡ Y= <

Here's How:

1. Write out your quotation, leaving space between each line for writing in the symbols above each letter. For example:

⌐⊓ ⌐⌐ ⊡⌐⌐⊐
H e i s r i s e n !

2. Make copies of the encoded quotation and the pigpen code for the students to use in deciphering the passage.

FOLLOW THE BOUNCING BALLS

Sometimes movies have encouraged the audience to join in community singing by projecting the text of a song with a bouncing ball moving along each line to indicate when each word should be sung. In this exercise, the words for a biblical text may be printed on a series of balls, with arrows and dotted lines indicating the movement.

Here's How:

1. Choose a biblical quotation, such as Psalm 100:1-2. Count the number of words in it.
2. Using a nickel or a quarter as a pattern, draw a circle for each word, arranging them in an attractive design on the page.
3. At random, write the quotation in the circles, using one word per circle.
4. Print "Start here" near the circle bearing the first word of the quotation. Use dotted lines and arrows to indicate the proper sequence of the words. Leave a space below for the students to write out the quotation as they discover it.
5. Give these directions: Follow the bouncing balls to read Psalm 100:1-2. Write the quotation on the lines below.

Try This:

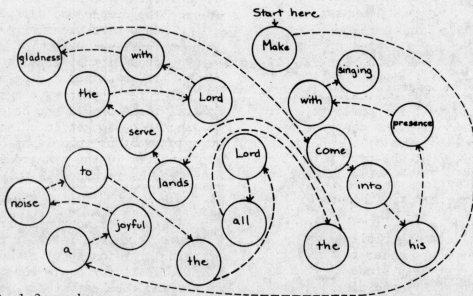

Psalm 100: 1-2 reads:

_____

_____

SONGS, HYMNS, AND ANTHEMS

Students remember what they sing, especially when the song has a strong melody and an interesting rhythm. Sometimes biblical texts, set to music, can be used to help students memorize the passages.

Here's How:

1. Supply your church's children and youth choir directors with a list of biblical texts you would like your students to learn. Ask if there are any anthems, service music, or hymns based on these texts that the choristers could learn and teach the other students.
2. Explore your denominational hymnal and some children's hymnals for songs and hymns using biblical texts (see Bibliography). Some hymnals have a scriptural index that will be helpful. Incorporate these songs and hymns in your teaching plans.
3. Check around in personal, public, school, and church libraries to see if there are any available choral recordings of hymns and anthems with biblical texts. Transfer individual hymns and anthems to cassette tape for a listening station or for use as a teaching aid with the total group.
4. Choreograph the musical setting of a biblical text for movement, using your own ideas or plans designed by others (see Bibliography). As the students interpret the text with their bodies, they will memorize it easily.

CHORAL SPEAKING

Reading or reciting biblical texts in unison or parts under the direction of a leader can help students commit the texts to memory and discover their meaning. In her book Twenty Ways to Use Drama in Teaching the Bible (see Bibliography), Judy Gattis Smith suggests that biblical texts may be arranged for choral speaking in a variety of ways.

Here's How:

1. Antiphonal readings are for two groups of equal voices who take turns speaking. The Hebrews of the Old Testament used this method when they recited many of the psalms in their worship.
2. Cumulative readings begin with one voice, but gradually add others on successive lines so that when the text reaches its climax the whole group is speaking in unison.
3. Line-around readings are arranged so that each person in the group has a line to read. The students stand in a circle in the order in which they speak so that the text flows around the circle from beginning to end.
4. Some texts may be arranged for a solo voice and chorus response. This approach is effective with some of the Old Testament psalms and prophecies that use the Hebrew way of writing an idea and then restating it in a second way. For example:
Solo: The people who walked in darkness have seen a great light;
Group: Those who dwelt in a land of deep darkness, on them has light shined. (Isaiah 9:2)
5. Other texts that have a strong central theme should not be divided, but should be spoken in unison. An example is Jesus' proclamation of his ministry in the synagogue at Nazareth, as recorded in Luke 4:18-19.

Try This:
1. Use tuned or nontuned percussion instruments to add interest to choral speaking; for instance, as appropriate sound effects for Psalm 150, as a means of keeping the beat steady, or as a way of giving certain words special meaning.
2. Use handbells to accompany the choral speaking. Select a basic key

for the text, such as G major. Assign all the G, B, and D bells available to students and suggest that they play their bells in random rhythmic patterns to introduce and conclude the text and at certain points throughout the reading.

RHYTHMIC SPEECH

Rhythmic speech adds a beat to choral speaking. Betty Ann Ramseth points out in That I May Speak (see Bibliography) that biblical texts can be learned more joyfully and more quickly when they are set to rhythm.

Here's How:

1. Select a text you want your students to memorize. For example, Galatians 5:22-23a: "The fruit of the Spirit is love, joy, peace, patience, kindness, goodness, faithfulness, gentleness, self-control."
2. Establish a steady beat by clapping your hands or beating a drum. Speak the text as you continue the beat. The natural accents of the words should fall on the beat. Try it different ways, and choose the one you like best. Establish a time signature and notate the rhythm above the words. For example:

3. See if you can lift out one short phrase that could be used as an ostinato, or repeated pattern, to accompany the reading. For example:

$\frac{6}{8}$ ‖:Fruit of the Spir-it.:‖

4. Divide the students into two groups. After you have established the beat with a drum or handclap, have one group begin repeating the ostinato pattern twice. Then as they continue this accompaniment pattern, have the rest of the group speak the entire text. Work for good phrasing, expression, and diction as you rehearse. Avoid a singsong effect.
5. Add tuned or nontuned percussion instruments as desired.

Try This:
Use biblical texts arranged for choral speaking and rhythmic speech as part of your worship, or share them with the congregation in special services.

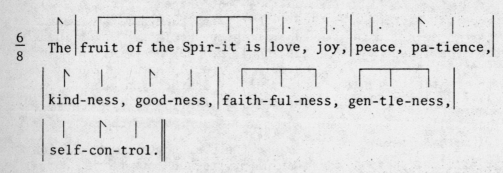

It's Happening All Over Again!

Students need opportunities to compare events in a Bible story with similar events happening today. God still is at work in the lives of people today!

CASE STUDIES OR OPEN-ENDED STORIES

Unfinished stories, based on biblical incidents but set in contemporary life situations, involve students in a problem-solving process that can help them discover the relevance of the Bible for life today.

Here's How:

1. Write an open-ended story based on a Bible story or biblical incident from your curriculum resources. For example, a story based on Jesus' encounter with Zacchaeus in Luke 19:1-10, could develop this plot:
    Maria was a girl no one liked. The other boys and girls in her room suspected that she was the one who had stolen Tim's lunch money from his desk. They knew the teacher had caught her cheating on tests more than once. One day when Susan was playing on the swings in the park, she saw Maria watching her. She sensed Maria was lonely and wanted to play with her. Susan didn't like Maria either, but she did feel sorry for her. It must be awful not to have any friends. Susan smiled at Maria and was just about to speak to her when she caught a glimpse of Margaret coming up the street. Margaret was the most popular girl in the class, and she had no time for Maria. What would Margaret say if she saw Susan playing with Maria? Susan decided . . .
2. Choose a way to share the story with your students: Tell it live, record it on cassette tape for a listening station, write it out on a story card, tell it with figures on a felt board, have a few of the students act out the incident for the others.
3. Help the students analyze the story by posing questions like these:
    List and describe the characters in the story.
    What are the problems facing the characters?
    Which is the most important?
    What are some possible solutions?
    Which is the best?
In addition to group discussion, students could be given the choice of offering solutions through informal dramatizations using masks

or hand puppets, role plays, written accounts, or drawings in various media. Be careful not to be judgmental so that the students will respond honestly. If you want to share your solution, offer it as another alternative, not the answer. Explore the consequences of all the alternatives with the students.

4. Have the students read the biblical incident on which the open-ended story was based. Ask the students to compare the two stories. How are they alike? How are they different? What was Jesus' solution? What were the consequences for Zacchaeus? For Jesus? How would Jesus' solution have worked for Susan?

GAMES AS DISCUSSION STARTERS

A game the students enjoy playing at home may be used in the classroom to relate key concepts from a Bible story to their everyday life. One game that could be used is Aggravation, which is manufactured by CO-5 Company, Inc.

Here's How:

1. Borrow the game of Aggravation from one of the students or a church family. Have it set up and ready to play when the students arrive.
2. Explain the game's rules, but then tell the students they may play it any way they want. Any actions will be acceptable. Let them play that way for about ten minutes.
3. Then suggest that the students play the game according to the rules you explained earlier for the same amount of time.
4. Ask the students which experience was more fun. Probably they will agree that the game was more fun when they followed the rules and knew what to expect. Suggest that they think of other areas in their lives where rules are good: family, school, traffic, athletics. Explain that

God has given us rules or laws to guide our behavior and bring order to our lives.
5. Use this discussion to introduce the concept of laws God gave to Israel through Moses as the people's part of the covenant.

PARAPHRASES

A paraphrase is a restatement of a biblical passage, giving the meaning in another form. Asking students to write paraphrases forces them to deal with the meaning of a biblical text in terms of their own experiences.

Here's How:

1. Choose a biblical passage that is of central importance to the concepts in your story or group of stories, such as the Ten Commandments from Exodus 20.
2. Plan for ways to involve the students in an intensive study of the passage: cassette tapes, reference books, worksheets, consultations with the teacher. They need to know what the passage meant to the people for whom it was written before they can paraphrase it.
3. Suggest that the students may work alone, in pairs, or as a total group on the paraphrase. If the passage can be easily divided into sections, each section could be assigned to a different person or pair, and their efforts could later be combined for a paraphrase of the whole.
4. Provide opportunities for the students to share their paraphrases in class or congregational worship, or in written form through the parish newsletter or a bulletin board display.

Try This:
Ask students to paraphrase the Ten Commandments in a positive form, as done by a group of fifth and sixth graders:

You shall worship me and only me.
You shall worship God, not yourselves
  or your friends, the things that you
  like to do, or the things that you
  want to have.
You shall say that you won't swear at
  all because you respect God's name.
Save some of your time to do things
  for God.
Show respect for your parents and
  love them.
You shall be kind to others and help,
  not hurt them.
You shall stay together with your
  husband or wife and be faithful to
  each other.
You shall leave things in the store
  unless you pay for them.
You shall tell the truth about your
  neighbor. You shall love your
  neighbor as yourself; share your
  things with him, care for him, not
  make him cry, not push him away,
  not gossip about him.
Be happy and content with what you
  have.

CARTOONS

Sometimes it is possible to find
cartoons in contemporary magazines
and newspapers that are related to
concepts in a Bible story. They may
be used in several ways in the
classroom.

Here's How:

1. Mount the cartoon on posterboard
and display it on a bulletin board to
stimulate discussion, provide insights
into biblical concepts, or share its
humor.
2. Enlarge the cartoon with the help
of an overhead projector, and use it
as the basis for a poster.
3. Remove the caption from the cartoon and ask the students, working
individually or in small groups, to
write original captions for it. Share

the various captions in group
discussion.
4. Change the original caption of the
cartoon to one more clearly relating
to the concepts in a Bible story.

OPEN-ENDED COMIC STRIPS

Comic strips from newspapers,
especially the longer strips from
Sunday comic sections, may be prepared
for use as open-ended stories for
discussion starters.

Here's How:

1. Choose an appropriate comic strip,
one with at least seven frames. Sometimes the first several frames will
pose a problem-situation relevant to
a Bible story your students are studying,
and the conversational balloons may be
left as they are. In other strips,
the dialogue may be irrelevant, but
the pictures will lend themselves to
other dialogue that can establish a
relevant problem-situation. In that
case, all the conversational balloons
will have to be removed.
2. Use a pair of scissors or X-acto
knife to cut out the conversational
balloons of the strip as necessary.
3. Glue the strip to a piece of
white paper with rubber cement so that
there will be new blank white balloons for the dialogue.
4. In the first several frames, use
the original dialogue or write in a
dialogue on the blank conversational
balloons to establish a problem
situation, leaving the rest of the
balloons blank.
5. Cover the mounted strip with
clear, self-adhesive vinyl, following
the directions in Better Media for
Less Money, pp. 30-31 (see Bibliography). Students may then use
water-soluble overhead projection
pens to write in the dialogue on the
rest of the frames to show how they
would solve the problem. When they
have shared their ideas, the dialogue

can be wiped off with a damp cloth, and the strip used again by other students.

CURRENT EVENTS

A common theme running through most of the stories in the Bible is God's loving actions in the lives of people and the response of people to these actions. This is also a common experience of people today. God acts, and people respond in one way or another. Newspapers and magazines are a record of the contemporary experience with God and can be used in the classroom to help students relate biblical events to events in their own time and place.

Here's How:

1. When students are learning about Old Testament prophets, give them a stack of newspapers and ask them to look for examples in which life today resembles life for the Hebrews during the prophetic period. Suggest that they use relevant headlines, pictures, articles, advertisements, comics, and other items to make a collage poster around the theme "Wanted: Prophets for Today."
2. Students may also search newspapers for signs of shalom, of life situations lived in harmony with God and with others, or stories of events that show people trying to follow the two commandments Jesus considered the greatest--love God, love your neighbor. Their findings could be shared in a bulletin board display. Magazines and radio and television newscasts can also be sources for relevant current events.
3. Watch for "living parables" in printed matter or television newscasts.

COMPARISON CARDS

A set of cards illustrated with contemporary examples of a concept important to a Bible story can help students discover the meaning of that concept.

Here's How:

1. Choose an important concept from a story or group of stories, such as "covenant."
2. Make a list of covenants made by people today. For example: 4-H pledge, Girl Scout Promise, baptismal vows, Hippocratic oath taken by medical doctors, Florence Nightingale pledge made by nurses, local church covenant, marriage vows, stewardship pledge to the church, pledge of allegiance to the flag, and a work contract between employer and employee. Obtain copies of the covenants and pictures of those persons involved. (Magazines, catalogs, Sunday bulletins, and old curriculum resources are good sources.)
3. Mount the illustrations for each covenant on a separate piece of posterboard, using the dry rubber cement method described in Better Media for Less Money, pp. 27-28.
4. Use the comparison cards in a bulletin board display or in a learning center to stimualte discussion on the meaning of covenant.

EXPERIMENTS

Simple scientific experiments with everyday materials can help students understand a story better.

Here's How:

1. Read Jesus' parable in which he compares the growth of the kingdom of God to the action of yeast in bread (Matthew 13:33).

2. Provide supplies for the students to set up three experiments:

    a. Knead a piece of thawed frozen bread dough, put it on an aluminum pie tin over a bowl of hot water, cover with a damp cloth, and let rise.

    b. Mix 1 package of active dry yeast with 1 teaspoon sugar and ¼ cup lukewarm water in a small bowl.

    c. Mix 1 tablespoon flour, 1 tablespoon lukewarm milk, and 1 tablespoon sourdough starter together in a bowl.

3. Move on to another activity while the leavening agents are working. At the end of the session, have the students observe what has happened. Explain that Jesus had noticed that a little bit of leaven caused bread to rise into a big loaf. He thought the kingdom of God would grow in the same way from something very small to something big.

Try This:
1. Look at a mustard seed under a microscope (Matthew 13:31-32).
2. Show uses of salt. Can you think why Jesus would have said we are the salt of the earth?

VICARIOUS EXPERIENCES

Opportunities to share vicariously in the experiences of others can be planned to help students discover the meaning of important biblical concepts.

Here's How:

1. Choose a concept, such as "trust."
2. Ask a visually handicapped person to share with the class (live or on cassette tape) the importance of trust to a person who is blind.
3. Plan some vicarious experiences of being blind for the students. For example:

    a. Outline a maze on the floor with masking tape. Blindfold the students (in another room so they don't see the maze), and ask them to find their way through the maze either by touch or by trusting the directions given by the leader.

    b. Set up an obstacle course, using chairs, large pillows, cardboard cartons, and similar objects. Ask for volunteers to try to negotiate the obstacle course, one at a time, while blindfolded. Give them each three chances. The first time, have them try to get through the course on their own. The second time, give them verbal directions. The third time, lead them by the hand safely through the course. Have the other students observe these attempts. Ask the blindfolded volunteers to express their feelings during each trip through the obstacle course. Invite the observers to share their reactions. Relate this experience to the concept of trust.

    c. Serve a light snack that requires the use of silverware and a drinking glass to students who are blindfolded and seated at a table. Ask them to trust your voice to help them find their food. After the students have shared their responses to these experiences, talk about the meaning of trust and what it means for them to trust God.

Try This:
1. Take the class to a park or landscaped yard. Just before entering, blindfold the students. Have one adult for every two students. Move around the park, touching and smelling, making note of how much more sensitive to detail (rough bark, velvety petals, spicy roots, shapes) persons are when they cannot see. Relate the experience to the concept of creation, giving thanks and appreciation to God as Creator. Help the students marvel at the way God has given people so many ways to experience and enjoy the world created for them.

2. Try a handicapped dinner. Plan a simple meal that will be served buffet style. Gather the students in another room. From a hat, have them draw slips of paper on which you have written descriptions of different physical handicaps, one per slip of paper. For example:
a. No hands
b. No hands or arms
c. No hands or arms with no sight
d. No legs
e. No legs and no arms
f. No sight
g. No tongue with no sight
h. Other handicaps
Provide paper and marking pens for the students to use in making signs to describe the handicaps they have drawn. For example: "I have no use of my hands and arms and am blind." Have the students wear the signs so they will be able to identify one another's handicaps. If desired, use strips of old sheets or old nylon stockings to immobilize limbs or blindfold students. When the food is ready and everyone is "handicapped," announce that the students should move into the dining area. Although there should be several leaders around for supervision, let the participants determine how the experience will develop. Probably they will eventually help one another as best they can, so that everyone can get to the dining room, be served, eat, and help clear the tables. Once the experience is over, suggest that the participants consider these questions:
a. What were some of the difficulties you had getting to the dining area? Obtaining your food? Eating your meal? Clearing the table?
b. What ways did you discover for helping one another get around these difficulties?

c. How did you feel about your inability to function in a normal way?
d. How did you feel toward others who needed help? Toward the leaders who had no handicaps?
e. What do you think handicapped persons need most?
Relate this discussion to the concept of Christian love, which includes both compassion and service. Have the students look up some incidents where Jesus healed handicapped persons in the Bible. What were their needs? How did Jesus show compassion for them and serve them? What other kinds of handicaps can people have (for example, Zacchaeus or the rich young ruler)? How did Jesus respond to them? Follow this with research into how persons from the historical and contemporary church life have met the needs of handicapped persons with compassion and service.

REAL EXPERIENCES

Carefully planned real-life experiences, followed by discussion, can help students relate concepts from a Bible story to their own lives.

Here's How:

1. Young students can discover the meaning of covenant by making rules for their class and promising to follow them.
2. By baking cookies together, students can learn the meaning of trust, as they trust the recipe, the oven temperature, their skill in mixing up the cookies, their equipment, and so forth.

SEE ALSO:
Skits with a Cast of Characters Box
Diamonte Poems

How Are They Related?

Students need to be encouraged to look at the relationships of people with one another and with God in a Bible story. They need to learn to ask: What insight does this story give us into our own relationships with God and one another?

SKITS WITH A CAST OF CHARACTERS BOX

Students may be helped to gain insight into the relationships among people in a Bible story by having them analyze similar relationships among people in contemporary life situations.

Here's How:

1. Read through the Bible story carefully, noting the kinds of relationships that exist among the characters. Which are crucial to an understanding of how God's love works in the lives of people to meet their needs? For example:

2. Find pictures in magazines, old curriculum resources, calendars, posters, and other sources to illustrate examples of the relationships you have identified in contemporary life. If you are unable to find illustrations of a particular relationship, you may be able to find pictures of persons who exhibit feelings that persons have in these relationships. Mount each picture separately on pieces of cardboard cut in free-form shapes. Use the dry rubber cement method described in Better Media for Less Money, pp. 27-28, and protect them as directed on pp. 30-31 (see Bibliography).

3. Find a cardboard carton large enough to hold the mounted pictures. Leaving the top open, cover the box with brightly colored self-adhesive vinyl or paper. Label the box

---

Joseph and his brothers	jealous, angry, violent, sorrowful, forgiving, reconciling
David and Jonathan	friendly, loyal, loving
Saul and David	jealous, loyal
Jesus and those he healed	compassionate, comforting, serving, loving, grateful
Zacchaeus and community	rejecting, dishonest, suspicious
Jesus and Zacchaeus	accepting, trusting, forgiving
Moses and Aaron	cooperative, sharing, trusting

"Cast of Characters." Place the pictures inside.

4. Use the Cast of Characters Box as a way of introducing the Bible story to the students. If you have included contemporary illustrations of relationships in the story, suggest that the students work in groups of two or three to choose a picture from the box and develop a skit to dramatize the situation illustrated and what they think will happen next. After the students have shared their skits, introduce the Bible story by saying that the people in the story found themselves in a situation very much like the people in their skits.

Or use the Cast of Characters Box as a way of helping the students reflect upon the relationships in the story. If you have used pictures illustrating feelings persons might have had in these relationships, ask the students to choose two or three kinds of pictures to use in making up a skit to indicate what kind of situations would have caused these feelings.

DIAMONTE POEMS

The diamonte poem has seven lines and contrasts a noun with its opposite, using the format below. The lines are worked on in the sequence indicated by the numbers:

Writing a diamonte poem requires students to describe God and an individual, or two individuals, and analyze their relationships to one another. The individuals may be characters from a Bible story or persons from contemporary life or both.

Here's How:

1. From a Bible story or group of Bible stories in a unit, choose persons who could be compared in a diamonte poem. (Be sure to include God!) List different combinations on a chalkboard, newsprint chart, or overhead transparency. For example, from the story of David you might list:
David and Jonathan
Saul and David
David and Absalom
David and Nathan
God and Saul
God and David
David and (own name)

2. Explain to the students that you want them to write a diamonte poem comparing two persons from the list. Go through the format and procedure for writing the poem. Suggest that they choose a pair from the list as the subjects for their poems.

3. Provide opportunities for the

---

1. Noun
3. Two words describing first noun
5. Three "ing" words that are action words related
to the first noun
7. A phrase uniting both nouns (line 1 and line 2)
6. Three "ing" words that are action words related to the second noun
4. Two words describing the second noun
2. Noun that is opposite of the first noun

For example:
Jonah
bad, selfish
hating, running, praying
a man and God.
loving, forgiving, helping
good, kind
God.

80

students to share their poems with
one another.

Try This:
Diamonte poems may also be used to
ask students to compare two related
concepts. For example:

Crucifixion
Jesus' death
Forgiving, suffering, dying
Crucifixion made Resurrection possible
Living, loving, saving
Jesus' life
Resurrection

STORY MAZE

A maze is a confusing, intricate
network of passages through which it
is difficult to find one's way. Although a puzzle in the form of a maze
is usually drawn out, it may also be
designed in the form of a story.

Here's How:

1. Use a Bible story that has a strong,
simple plot. Identify points in the
story where the major character has to
make decisions of importance.
2. Rewrite the story in your own words,
stopping each time the character is
faced with a decision. List three
possible choices of action for the
character to take, one of which should
be the decision made in the story.
The other two choices should be
ridiculous alternatives or decisions
that would obviously lead to disastrous
results.
3. Set up the story in booklet form,
using one-fourth of an 8½" x 11" sheet
of paper for each page. Plan one page
for each situation (the part of the
story leading up to another decision),
and one page for each of the three
alternatives for every decision-
making situation. Begin with a title
page and one for giving directions.
For example:
This maze will take you through the

story of Nehemiah if you choose the
correct answer for each situation
that is described. Begin with
Situation 1 on page 3, and follow
the directions as given. Each
correct answer will lead you to the
next situation. Each incorrect
answer will make it necessary for you
to return to the situation and try
again. Biblical references are given
for each situation, in case you want
to use them.
Then arrange the other pages so that
they are not at all in logical order.
Number the pages consecutively. At
the bottom of each situation page,
list the alternative choices and the
page where each one leads. The right
choice should lead to the next situation in the story. The other choices
should lead to pages explaining why
they are wrong decisions and directing
them to return to the situation and
try another alternative. For example:
Situation 1 (Nehemiah 1)
    Although he was a Jew, Nehemiah
had always lived in Persia. His
ancestors had been captured and
brought there from Jerusalem when
the city was burned and the Temple
destroyed. In recent years, some
Jews had returned to Jerusalem, but
Nehemiah had stayed in his good
position as a servant to the king.
Then came bad news from Jerusalem.
The Temple was being rebuilt, but
the walls of the city were in ruins.
It could easily be attacked.
Nehemiah listened to the news and
a. decided there was nothing to worry
   about because walls were old-
   fashioned anyway.
b. sat down and cried.
c. went to the king and asked for
   permission to go to Jerusalem
   himself to help rebuild the wall.
If you chose (a), go to p. 8.
If you chose (b), go to p. 10.
If you chose (c), go to p. 5.
Page 8: You have selected an incorrect
   answer for Situation 1. Walls were
   necessary around a city to protect

its citizens from their enemies. No city could grow strong without a wall. Go back to page 3 and try another answer.

Page 10: This answer is only partially correct. He did sit down and cry, but did not stop with this.

Page 5: (Situation 2 is described.)

4. Use the story maze after the students have become acquainted with the story in other ways.

OBITUARY

An obituary is a notice of a death with a biographical sketch of the deceased. Within a traditional format, which is often printed in a newspaper and read as part of the funeral service, basic information about the life of the deceased and his or her special accomplishments is shared. Writing obituaries for characters from Bible stories can help students reflect upon their lives and identify what was important about them, especially in terms of their relationships to God and one another.

Here's How:

1. Choose major Bible characters for this project, such as Moses, David, Solomon, Amos, Jeremiah, Nehemiah, Jesus, Paul, Sarah, Deborah, Lydia.

2. Develop a format for an obituary based on biographical data the students will be able to find on the character, and include statements that will help them focus on what was important in their lives. For example:

_____, age ____, died today from____.
He (she) is survived by_____.
He (she) was a member of_____.
At the time of death, he (she) was ____
_____.
The deceased will be remembered for
_____.
and will be mourned by_____.
The body will be _____.
Instead of flowers, memorials are preferred to _____.

3. Ask the students to use the format to write an obituary for the character you select. Give them the option of working individually or in pairs.

4. Provide an opportunity for students to share their obituaries and discuss them. How are they alike? How are they different? What was the most important thing the Bible character did? Why do people still remember him or her?

NEW TEXTS FOR OLD TUNES

One way to have students indicate their insight into the nature of the relationships of people in Bible stories to one another and to God is to have them write original lyrics for familiar rounds and fun songs like:
"Row, Row, Row Your Boat"
"Are You Sleeping?"
"Old MacDonald Had a Farm"
"Mary Had a Little Lamb"
"Sweetly Sings the Donkey"
For example:

God's Call to Jonah
(To the tune:
"Row, Row, Row Your Boat")
Go to Nineveh,
And preach to all those there:
I am the God who cares, loves, and forgives.
Don't fret and pull your hair.

To Jonah in the Boat
(To the tune: "Are You Sleeping?")
Are you sleeping? Are you sleeping?
Selfish man, selfish man.
God is looking for you,
God is looking for you.
There he ran. There he ran.

Here's How:

1. Post a newsprint chart or give the students a worksheet with some kind of diagram indicating the format for the song. For example, the format for "Row, Row, Row Your Boat" would be:

— — — — — (5 syllables)
— — — — — (5 syllables)
— — — — — (12 syllables)
— — — — — (5 syllables)

2. Decide on the rhyme scheme. (In this round, the last words in lines 2 and 4 rhyme.)

3. Talk about some possible ideas for the song. Who is speaking and to whom: God? A character from the story? The writer? What feelings are involved? What actions? What is happening when the song is sung?

4. Give the students time to write. Be available if they want to try out their ideas on you. Make suggestions and help them when necessary, but let the work be theirs. Encourage the students to work together if they like.

5. Make the texts available to all the students and provide an opportunity for them to have the fun of singing the new songs together.

SIMULATED EXPERIENCES

Students can gain insight into the relationships of people in the Bible to God and to one another by participating in simulated or staged experiences in the classroom that correspond to biblical events. For example, experiences could be planned to help students discover several factors involved in a covenant relationship.

Here's How:

1. *An experience of choosing and being chosen.* Choose two students to select six to ten persons (depending on the size of your group) each for a spelldown. After they have made their choices, explain that you were mistaken about the activity. There will be a kickball game instead of a spelldown. Ask them if they want to keep the same sides or choose over. Accept their decision without comment. Then confer with another teacher and announce that instead of a kickball game, there will be a beauty contest. Offer the captains the option again of keeping the same sides or choosing over. After they have responded, raise these questions: Why do we make the choices we do? Why are we chosen or not chosen? Let the students share their ideas, and then comment that sometimes we choose and are chosen because there is a job for us to do, not because we have any particular qualifications or abilities.

2. *An experience of being part of an agreement.* In advance, assign all the students, according to their needs and abilities, to specific tasks related to Bible stories where the concept of covenant is important. The assignments should be written on individual cards containing a brief description of the task and a pledge to be signed by a teacher and the student. Distribute the cards, explaining that although the students will not be allowed to trade tasks, they do have the option of not signing the agreement. Those who choose not to be a part of the agreement will go to a different room than those who agree to work on their assignments.

3. *An experience of being loyal to one another and to their common task.* Encourage those who chose to be part of task groups to work together until their tasks are finished.

4. *An experience of being outside the agreement.* Arrange for those who decided not to agree to a task to meet in a room bare of all materials and equipment. Have a teacher meet with them, but exert no leadership except to explain that they are free to do whatever they want with whatever they have brought into the room with them. Near the end of the time allotted for this experience, invite them to share their reactions. (One group reported that choosing to reject an assignment had made them feel guilty and had left them without a purpose. They were bored without any-

thing to do, and finally started to sing. They felt cut off from those who had agreed to their assignments.)

5. *Reflection*. At the end of the session, gather all the students together and ask each task group to share their work on an overhead transparency. Have the students who chose not to agree to a task share their experience. Then project a transparency on which you have written the word "covenant." Ask the students to identify some of the factors involved in any covenant, and write them on the transparency:

choice	who takes part in the agreement
promise	what each party agrees to do
relationships	how this affects interaction between parties
loyalty	what is required for the agreement to succeed

Conclude by asking students to think of covenant relationships in which persons are involved today.

PAINT YOUR FEELINGS

Sometimes students relate to the way Abraham, Moses, or another Bible person felt when experiencing life and making decisions, but cannot express their feelings verbally or in writing. Encourage them to try painting their feelings. Color, strokes, and design can say a lot.

Here's How:

1. Provide large sheets of manila paper on easels, or have the students work on tables or the floor.
2. Mix several colors of powdered tempera with water and a little powdered or liquid detergent. (The detergent makes the paint easy to clean up afterwards.)
3. Cut a 4 5/8" x 3" x 11/16" sponge into six sticks. The students can use the corners, flat sides, and sharp edges of the sponge sticks for daubing and various line strokes.
4. Ask the students to paint how they think a Bible character felt at one or more crucial times in life--for instance, Moses when he was growing up in Pharaoh's court, when he saw the Hebrews being beaten, when God called him to lead the Hebrews out of Egypt or Jesus when he was tempted or baptized.

Try This:
Ask the students to paint how they feel when they are happy, sad, angry, confused, or peaceful, and then match this feeling to one experienced by the Bible character. Have them share their work with one another.

SEE ALSO:
Vicarious Experiences

What Does God Have to Do with All This?

Students need a chance to respond to the way God has spoken to them through the Bible story. They need to learn ways to share their faith with one another. They need to learn how to communicate with God in prayer.

CHRISTMAS CARDS AS A DISCUSSION STARTER

Christmas cards may be recycled for an exercise designed to help students think about the nature of God's love.

Here's How:

1. Collect a group of Christmas cards portraying the Nativity story in different cultures. (Cards produced by UNICEF are a good source.)
2. Display the cards on a bulletin board, or mount them for a Pick-a-Picture Box (see Index).
3. Give these directions: Most of the early followers of Jesus were Jews who followed the laws of that faith even after they became Christians. As the church was organized, it began to attract Gentiles who did not follow the Jewish laws. The question arose: Do Gentile Christians also have to follow the Jewish laws to be a part of the church? Christians who had been Pharisees said yes. Peter, Paul,

Barnabas, James, and others said no. With which group would the artists of these pictures agree? Why? Which side won out? (See Acts 15:23-29.) (The artists would agree with the no vote, because they have portrayed Jesus as belonging to all cultures, as coming for all people everywhere, not just those who follow the Jewish laws. This is the position that won out in the early church. God's love is for everyone, not just a few.)

OPINION BOX

Students are more likely to give honest responses to questions and issues if they are able to do so anonymously, without worrying about how their teacher or fellow students will react. An Opinion Box enables them to think about a question, write an answer on a card, and deposit it in a box along with those from other students. Since the cards are never signed, they can be removed and used as the basis for discussion without revealing the identity of each writer.

Here's How:

1. Cover a cardboard box (such as a shoe box) and lid with wrapping paper

or colored, self-adhesive vinyl. Label
the box "Opinion Box." Cut a slot in
the lid wide enough to receive 3" x 5"
cards.

2. Provide a stack of cards and
pencils for the students to use for
writing their opinions.

Try This:

1. Use the Opinion Box along with other
resources in a learning center. For
example, display a group of mounted
magazine pictures illustrating human
suffering or a group of pictures showing human love and concern for others.
Give these directions: Look at the
pictures. What does God have to do
with all these situations? Write
your opinion on the card and put it
in the Opinion Box.

2. Use the Opinion Box when the whole
class is working with an open-ended
story, especially if it is one that
asks for personal decisions about
their own behavior. It will enable
students to answer more honestly such
questions as: What do you think God
would want you to do? What would you
really do? Group discussion can then
focus on problems we share in trying
to follow God's way of love, rather
than on pat answers.

3. Suggest that the students use a
format for their opinions to indicate
how their thinking may have changed
as a result of their experiences in
class. For example:

> I used to think . . .
> but now I know . . .

GRAFFITI BOARD

Graffiti are inscriptions or drawings
made on a rock or wall. A graffiti
board is a display area especially
designed for people to use for writing
their ideas about concepts from a Bible
story, their feelings about God, their
hopes and dreams for God's kingdom, or
their response to any number of questions posed by the teacher.

Here's How:

1. Cover a bulletin board with brown
wrapping paper or newsprint or paint
a large cardboard carton a bright,
light color or cover it with paper or
use a white board or chalkboard. Allow
ample space for the students to write
or draw. Provide chalk or marking pens
in several colors.

2. Give directions that ask the students to respond to a specific question
by writing or drawing on the graffiti
board.

Try This:

1. Make a Graffiti Gift Box from a
large cardboard carton by painting
it and decorating it with a large
Christmas bow. On one side, write
the third stanza of "O Little Town
of Bethlehem," which begins "How
silently, how silently the wondrous
gift is given." On the other three
sides, ask the students to write or
draw some "silent" gifts they could
give to thank God for the gift of
Jesus. (For example: a hug, a
smile, love, forgiveness, friendship,
worship.)

2. When students are working with
stories about David, use the graffiti
board to ask them to complete this
statement: "David and Jonathan were
friends. A friend is . . ." Decorate
the outer edges of the graffiti board
with brief statements illustrating their
friendship: "Jonathan saved David's
life," "David cared for Jonathan's
son," and others. Provide a Bible
storybook where the students can read
a short illustrated account of the
friendship.

SENTENCE PRAYERS

Writing original prayers of one sentence offers students an opportunity
to respond to God in a simple, direct
way. It is an experience that can
help them learn the discipline of

prayer and how to use prayer in everyday life situations.

Here's How:

1. Plan how to motivate your students to write original prayers. For example, if they have been learning about how Jesus taught the disciples to pray, explain that the people of Jesus' day were not used to making up their own prayers. Jesus taught them that we can pray to God at any time, and God will always listen. Ask the students to list all the times they can think of when people could pray. For example: at the beginning of the day, at mealtime, at the end of the day, when people are sick or sad, when your enemies hurt you, when you have something hard to do.

2. Suggest that the students write sentence prayers for situations you have described on 3" x 5" cards in a Times for Prayer Box (a recipe file). For example:

Situation: Your mother has cooked your favorite food and you are really hungry tonight.
Prayer: Thank you, God, for this good food and for Mother who has taken the time to cook it. Amen.

Situation: You have just awakened, and remember the test facing you at school today. You've studied hard, but you're worried.
Prayer: Dear God, help me to do my best today. Amen.

3. Have the students share their prayers with you and one another. Use this time to help them grow in their understanding of the nature of prayer. Some students may be unrealistic in their petitions; for example, praying "Help me get an A" instead of "Help me do my best." Others may need help in showing thankfulness for persons through whom God has worked; for instance, "Thank you for the food"

but forgetting to thank God for the person who prepared it, the farmers who grew it, and so forth.

Try This:

1. To help students write prayers of thanksgiving to God, fill a Pick-a-Picture Box (see Index) with mounted pictures illustrating God's many gifts: healthy bodies, food, homes, church, school, natural beauty, seasons, parents, grandparents, children, babies, pets, teachers, jobs, the Bible, Jesus. Ask the students to look through the pictures, select one or more that best illustrates God's gifts to them, and write a prayer thanking God for them. If you use this exercise at Thanksgiving time, decorate a bulletin board with a large construction paper cornucopia and the words "Thank you, God." Have the students write their prayers on different colored construction paper shapes in the forms of fruits and vegetables and display them with the cornucopia on the bulletin board.

2. Whenever possible, incorporate the prayers the students have written into your classroom worship services. Or print a collection of the prayers to share with the students' families or members of the congregation.

COMPOSITE PRAYERS

A class or small group may want to write a prayer together with the help of a teacher. Such a prayer should be developed around a central theme or concept or in response to a specific situation.

Here's How:

1. Choose a theme for your prayer that is related to experiences your students have shared.

2. Explain the different parts of a prayer: adoration or praise, confession and asking for forgiveness,

petitions for others or yourselves, thanksgiving.

3. Decide if the students want to work on the prayer as a total group or work on assigned parts individually or in pairs.

4. Develop the prayer, using suggestions from the total group for each section or combining the sections written by individuals or pairs.

5. Use the prayer in your classroom worship.

LITANIES

A litany is a prayer consisting of a series of statements by a leader, alternating with one or several different responses repeated by the total group. It is a good format to use when composing a prayer with a group of students and is effective in worship because it allows for everyone to participate.

Here's How:

1. Decide on a specific theme for the prayer. For example, litanies could be composed asking God's help for times when we are afraid or thanking God for the world God has created or praying that God will help various persons in need.

2. Working with an overhead projector or a newsprint chart, ask the students to suggest ideas for the prayer. Explain that the litany can include all the elements of prayer (adoration, confession, petition, thanksgiving) or just develop one of them.

3. Group the ideas together according to their content. Each statement for the leader may include several ideas or sentences. Decide if you can use the same response after each statement or will need several responses.

4. Choose one or more appropriate responses as needed. Depending on the content of the statements, the students may write their own responses, select a biblical passage as a response (e.g., Psalm 107:1), or use a refrain from a hymn (e.g., "For the Beauty of the Earth"). The latter could be read or sung.

5. Use the prayer in your classroom worship.

Try This:

1. Develop a litany from a group of sentence prayers students have written earlier.

2. Develop a litany from responses students have written on a graffiti board.

TURN-AROUND PRAYERS

A turn-around prayer is a sentence prayer in which the first part of the sentence acknowledges a blessing the students enjoy and the second part of the sentence recognizes that there are some who do not share in that blessing. It is a prayer that is meaningful to use when students are involved in special giving or service projects in the church.

Here's How:

1. Suggest that the students make a list of all the blessings they enjoy from God.

2. Opposite each idea on the list, ask the students to describe what life is like for persons who do not share in that blessing.

3. Have the students choose one of these ideas and its opposite and use it in writing a turn-around prayer. The format of the prayers should be:
When I (state blessing), O God, help me to (remember those who don't share in blessing).
Have some examples ready to share before the students begin to work:
When my friend and I have fun outside together, O God, help me to think about the children who have no friends.

When my mother cooks my favorite dish and I eat until I am stuffed, O God, help me to remember the children who have no food to eat tonight.

TELEPHONE PRAYER

At times, prayers sound like telephone conversations, with God on one end of the line and persons on the other. This idea can be used as the basis for some informal dramatizations used to stimulate discussion on prayer. It will help students discover that different kinds of conversations are like different kinds of prayers.

Here's How:

1. Obtain two play telephones and set them up on opposite sides of the room. Have a battery-operated radio ready for use.
2. Choose four students for the skits, one to play God and the other three to pretend they are persons making calls to God.
3. Give the students these directions cards:
God -- React to each phone call as you think God would react.
Caller 1 -- Call God about a problem, describing it quickly with great detail. Ask for help, but don't give God a chance to comment. Hang up and rush off before God has a chance to answer.
Caller 2 -- Recite the Lord's Prayer in a monotonous voice. Hang up when you are finished. Don't give God a chance to answer.
Caller 3 -- Turn up the radio to top volume. Pretend there is a verbal fight going on in the background. Attempt to talk to God, but keep stopping as if you are interrupted by the radio and those talking in the background. Finally hang up in disgust.
4. Talk with the students about their roles, and help them plan what they will say. (Older youth can probably act out the roles spontaneously without any help.)
5. Before the students put on the skits for the rest of the class, explain that prayer is talking with God. Since we can't see God, it's a little like talking over the telephone. The students will demonstrate some ways we talk with God.
6. After the skits are finished, ask the students to compare the conversations with prayer. How were they alike? How were they different? What is real prayer?

WRITING A STATEMENT OF FAITH

Writing a statement of faith at the end of a unit or term can be a valuable exercise for students because it forces them to reflect upon their experiences with the Bible in the context of the Christian community and requires them to make some decisions about what they believe.

Here's How:

1. Give the students a specific topic. Ask them to write what they believe about God, Jesus Christ, the Holy Spirit, or concepts related to your curriculum.
2. Help the students decide how they want to work. There are several options:
Students may work individually, with each person writing a personal statement.
Students may work individually, but combine their personal ideas into a composite statement.
Students may work as a group to write a statement of faith, with a teacher acting as a recorder and another leading the discussion.
3. Share the statements of faith that result with the congregation in a worship service or bulletin board display or in a church newsletter.

CINQUAINE POEMS

A cinquaine poem is a five-line stanza that develops a single concept, using this format:

Line 1 -- A single concept word

Line 2 -- Two words describing the concept

Line 3 -- Three words of action telling about the concept

Line 4 -- Four words expressing feelings for the concept

Line 5 -- One word that restates the concept

For example:

Prophet
Truthful teller
Speaks for God
Courageous, Wise, honest, faithful,
Daniel

Prophet
God's servant
Proclaims God's plan
Feared, admired, respected, rejected
Spokesman

Students may express their ideas about God in cinquaine poems that use "God" as the first line.

Here's How:

1. Ask the students to list what they have discovered about God from the Bible story or group of stories they have been studying.

2. Explain the format of the cinquaine poem to them, using an overhead projector, newsprint chart, or chalkboard. Suggest that they write a cinquaine poem about God, using ideas from their list. Have several dictionaries and a thesaurus ready for reference. Give the students the option of working individually or in pairs.

3. Provide an opportunity for the students to share their poems in a read-aloud session, on a bulletin board, or in a printed form.

HAIKU AND SENRU POEMS

These Japanese poetry forms each use seventeen syllables, distributed as follows:

Line 1 -- 5 syllables

Line 2 -- 7 syllables

Line 3 -- 5 syllables

The haiku poem is a single thought related to nature and one of the four seasons. The senru poem is a single observation on any subject, with no reference to nature. The latter is probably more useful in church settings, except for units on God's creative activity. Here are two senru poems about anger, written by second and third graders:

When we get mad we
throw things at our walls and tear
our pillows and cry.

Anger is to be
mad at someone. But God wants
us all to forgive.

These simple poetry forms offer students a format for expressing a single idea about God, based on their experiences with a Bible story or group of stories. (The format, of course, may also be used by the students to make observations about concepts from a story or their own related everyday experiences.)

Here's How:

1. Ask the students to share what they have discovered about God in the story. Record their observations on an overhead transparency, chalkboard, or newsprint chart.

2. Display and explain the format for haiku and senru poems. Suggest that they use the format to express one of the ideas about God on their list.

3. Provide opportunities for the students to share the poems with one another.

CONCRETE POEMS

A concrete poem is a shaped poem in which the words themselves form an outline or fill in an outline of a shape related to the poem's content. For example:

The concrete poem challenges students to express their ideas about God or persons in Bible stories or key concepts from the stories in both words and pictures.

GOD CALLS JONAH TO PREACH TO HIS FOES. IN THE OPPOSITE DIRECTION OFF HE GOES. GOD SENDS A STORM AND A GREAT BIG FISH. JONAH TURNS AROUND AND FOLLOWS GOD'S WISH. "NINEVEH, REPENT AND CHANGE YOUR WAYS, OR GOD WILL DESTROY YOU AND END YOUR DAYS."

Here's How:

1. Choose a theme for the poems and suggest several simple shapes that might be relevant. For example:

Jonah   A large fish or whale
Moses   Stone tablets
Jesus   Cross in any one of
          many forms
David   Crown

Make cardboard patterns for these shapes.

2. Discuss the theme with the students. Have them share their ideas about the theme, and consider how they could be used in their poems.

3. Suggest that the students pencil in a shape on plain white paper before beginning to write. They may use one of the cardboard patterns you have prepared or a design of their own. Caution them to keep the design simple. Explain that the phrases do not have to rhyme, although they may.

4. When the poems are finished, have the students cut them out and mount them on colored construction paper or posterboard for display. Encourage them to share their work with one another.

Try This:

A simpler approach is to choose a symbol for an event in a story and sketch it on shelf paper or newsprint. Have the students make a list of key words in the passage and use these words to outline or fill in the symbol. For example, the butterfly could be a symbol for Easter. Key words for the poem could be joy, sunrise, new day, Alleluia, new life. Or, key words from the story of the feeding of the five thousand (five thousand, Jesus, disciples, blessed, ate, satisfied, baskets) could be used to outline or fill in a sketch of five loaves and two fish.

WORD BADGES

Sometimes there seems to be a button for every occasion imaginable: high school and college homecomings, political campaigns, centennial celebrations, fan clubs, and many others. Why shouldn't buttons be used in the church? Students of all ages can make their own buttons to express their ideas about God or about people in Bible stories.

Here's How:

1. Check with your school or local chamber of commerce to see if they will give you leftover, outdated buttons. Or ask families in your congregation to donate old buttons.

2. Make several cardboard circle patterns, 3/4 to 1 inch wider in diameter than the buttons. Obtain self-adhesive vinyl in several colors, and cut it in squares to fit the patterns.

3. Give these directions: Choose a pattern a little larger than your button. Trace around it on the wrong side of the vinyl. (In case a pencil slips, it won't be noticeable.) Use a scissors to cut out the circle. Peel off the backing, and lay the circle sticky-side up on a table. Place the button upside down on the vinyl circle. Pick up the button, and press the vinyl down, smoothing out all the air bubbles, working from the center out. With scissors, slash the vinyl from its outer edge to the edge of the button at ¼-inch intervals all around the button, so the vinyl can be folded and overlapped to the back of the button. Use permanent markers to write a message on the button, decorating it as desired. Spray the finished button lightly with clear acrylic to ensure the permanence of the design. (Too much spray may cause it to run.) Some sample messages from the story of Jonah:

God loves Jonahs!
God loves everyone!
I am Jonah's fan!
I am God's fan!
You can't run away from God!

4. Encourage the students to wear the buttons home. It will give them an opportunity to share the insights they have gained into the character of God from the story with their families.

RHYTHM MONTAGE

A montage is made by combining several different ideas or pictures attractively on a backing to illustrate a common theme or concept. A rhythm montage uses sounds, rhythms, words, and music instead of visual materials to accomplish the same purpose. Students can use the rhythm montage to express their ideas about God or about characters in Bible stories or to describe and give examples of specific concepts, such as love, giving thanks, or friendship.

Here's How:

1. Choose a person or concept for the theme of the rhythm montage. If it is a person, ask the students to list all the things that the person is and does. For example:
God is love.
God is wise.
God forgives.
God asks us to serve one
  another in love.
If the theme is a concept, have the students describe it in different ways (for example, giving thanks is showing appreciation), give examples (giving thanks is a happy face), and tell how they feel about it (giving thanks is a joyful task). Record the students' ideas on an overhead transparency, chalkboard, or newsprint chart.

2. Depending on the size of your class, have the students individually or in small groups choose phrases from your list that express ideas they think are important. Establish a basic beat on a drum or with a handclap, and suggest that the students practice saying their phrases rhythmically in different ways until they find one that they like. Have a variety of tuned and nontuned percussion instruments available for them to use with their phrases as they like.

3. Gather the students in a circle, and ask them to share how they have decided to speak their phrases. Help them decide how to combine them; for example, with each part spoken in turn, added one by one as others continue, or entering and ending at different points like a canon or round. Have them think about adding a phrase from a hymn as one of the parts. For example:

(Note: The leader will establish the beat with a hand drum, giving eight counts before the speaking begins. The lines enter in the order indicated and speaking is continued until all the lines have entered. Then the refrain is sung in unison, to the tune of "Nun Danket," first line only.)

4. Use the rhythm montage in your classroom worship.

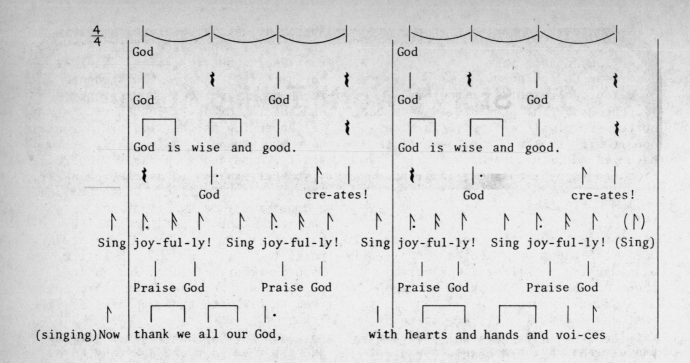

The Story's Worth Telling Again

A good story is always worth repeating! When a story has had meaning for students, they need a chance to tell it to others in a creative, exciting way.

CHARADES

Charades is an old parlor game that involves some miming and guessing. It is a good method for reviewing and retelling Bible stories.

Here's How:

1. Write scenes from Bible stories on separate sheets of paper. Fold the slips and put them in a basket.
2. Divide the group into teams of two or three.
3. The teams take turns drawing slips and acting out scenes while the others try to guess what they are portraying. (No guesses allowed until the scene is finished!)

Try This:
1. Have teams write out words or proper nouns for the opposing team to mime. One player draws a slip, reads it, and acts out the whole word or syllables for his teammates until they guess the correct answer. Teams alternate turns.

2. If events are used, then the whole team chooses one and acts it out for the opposing team to guess.

TELLING A STORY WITH PICTURES

Younger children can be helped to retell a Bible story with pictures and a felt board.

Here's How:

1. Decorate a cardboard box, label it "Picture-Story Box," and fill it with pictures illustrating a Bible story. Use prints photographed from a curriculum book or picture-book version of the story, mounted pictures of persons from a contemporary catalog who would represent Bible characters to the children, or mounted drawings you have had someone do of the characters. Each picture should have felt or nonwoven interfacing glued on its back so it will adhere to a feltboard. Directions for making a felt board may be found in Better Media for Less Money, p. 24 (see Bibliography).
2. Invite a student to choose three pictures from the box and arrange them on the felt board. Then help the student decide who the characters

are and use them in telling an incident from the story.

NEW SCRIPTS FOR OLD FILMSTRIPS

Sometimes it pays to save a filmstrip version of a Bible story until after the students have become familiar with it in other ways. Then let them use their knowledge of the story to view the filmstrip without any recorded narration and write their own script.

Here's How:

1. Plan a variety of experiences with a Bible story for the students so they will become familiar with the plot and characters.
2. Show them a filmstrip version of the story without any recorded or spoken narration. Suggest that they explain what is happening instead.
3. Ask the students to view the filmstrip again, this time writing down a brief narration or dialogue for each frame.
4. Show the filmstrip again, using the student-prepared script.

WRITE-ON SLIDES, FILMSTRIPS, FILMS

Students can retell a story in a biblical or contemporary setting by designing and making their own slide show. They can use scripture for their script or write their own interpretation of the story.

Here's How:

1. Choose a story, and block out the scenes to be illustrated. Assign the students to the scenes, or let them choose.
2. Provide the necessary materials. Write-on slides and filmstrips may be purchased from Griggs Educational Service (see Bibliography), or you can make your own, as follows:
    a. Purchase cardboard slide mounts and sheets of cellulose acetate. Cut the acetate sheets into 1½" x 1¼" pieces. Fit the pieces into mounts and seal them with a warm iron.
    b. Use a strong solution of chlorine bleach and water to clean an outdated filmstrip so it can be used as a write-on filmstrip by the students. For drawing, use special pens or pencils (available from Griggs), permanent or water-soluble overhead transparency pens, ordinary lead pencils, Fiddle-sticks pens.
3. Have the students sketch their drawings in 1-inch squares on white drawing paper. Then they can lay their slides over the sketches and trace the drawing on them. Stick figures, words, and symbols may be used.
4. Students can prepare the script, following the ideas on page
5. Arrange for the students to share their production with another class, their parents, or the congregation.

Try This:
1. Include other kinds of slides in the production. For example, outdated, damaged, or poor filmstrips may be recycled by cutting them apart into single frames and mounting them in holders. Picture-lift slides, described in detail in the following section, may also be used.
2. Have students record their script on tape, along with special music.
3. For a different effect, experiment with scratching lines and words on black exposed film that has been cut and mounted in slide holders.
4. Negatives can also be used for a special effect.

PICTURE-LIFT SLIDES

The ink from small colored pictures (approximately 1½ inches square) printed on clay-base paper may be lifted and deposited on transparent plastic, placed in a slide mount, and projected with a slide projector. A group of such slides could be used by students to retell a Bible story, such as the story of creation, or a biblical story in a modern setting.

Here's How:

1. Prepare a group of picture-lift slides, using the process described in Better Media for Less Money, pp. 39-41. Follow the directions there, except use Scotch-brand book tape #845 for the lifts. Slide mounts are available from Griggs Educational Service (see Bibliography). National Geographic magazines printed before 1973 are a good source for pictures. Choose those that relate to the story the students will retell. (Older students will enjoy making the picture-lift slides themselves.)
2. Display the slides on a slide sorter or an overhead projector. Let the students select those that they feel best illustrate the story and number them in the order in which they will be used.
3. Have the students write a brief script or captions for the slides they have selected. Use the slides and script in your classroom worship or sharing time.

DRAMATIZED MUSICALS

In recent years there have been many musicals based on Bible stories written for children's and youth choirs to perform in the church, either in a concert version or as a dramatic production complete with costumes, props, backdrops, and lighting. Some of these musicals are good, but others are of lesser quality. (Check the Bibliography for a listing of suitable musicals.) If you contemplate using a musical with your students, check it carefully to see that the text is faithful to the biblical account and is well written. If there is a re-cording available, listen to the music to see if it is of good quality in terms of strong melodies, appealing rhythms, and interesting accompaniments. Are there musicians in the church who could handle the accompaniments? If not, is an accompaniment tape available and within the budget? Consider how the musical could be staged and costumed. Would you dramatize the musical or do it in the concert version? Is there a royalty fee?
If you find a musical you feel is suitable, be brave and do it! Students of all ages will enjoy retelling a Bible story in this way and will remember that story all their lives.

Here's How:

1. Enlist the help of the children's or youth choir director in your congregation so the students can begin learning the music as part of their regular rehearsals several months in advance of the scheduled performance.
2. Sign up all the instrumentalists you can find among the teen-agers and adults in the church. It's nicer to do accompaniments live, if you can. Listen to the recording as you read the score, and note where you can add the other instruments available to the basic piano accompaniment. Tuned and nontuned percussion instruments, English handbells, autoharp, piano melodica, recorder, flute, oboe, cornet, violin, string bass, baritone horn, guitar, and a drum set are all possibilities.
3. Recruit other teen-agers and adults to paint backdrops using latex paint on sections of brown or white wrapping paper butted together and fastened with masking tape on the reverse side. Ask their help in designing props and making costumes. Borrow a spotlight, and find someone to run it.
4. Plan how this experience will be related to their classroom experiences. One church has produced several dramatized musicals through its annual

vacation church school sessions. The teachers develop a curriculum around concepts from the Bible story, using the learning center approach. The children's choir director rehearses the music several weeks in advance. During vacation church school, the students spend mornings in the class-room and the afternoons in rehearsing the production or working on related projects such as making banners, pre-paring program covers, and constructing props. Nonsingers are given parts in the production that don't involve singing. The musical is shared with the congregation at the annual Children's Day service at the end of the week.

Other churches have produced drama-tized musicals with an intergenerational group formed for that purpose. For six to eight weeks they meet together to learn more about the Bible story and rehearse the production. Some have incorporated dramatized musicals into their regular church school or released time programs for specific periods of time. Still others, feeling they were too short on leadership and participants to undertake a production on their own, have been joined by one or more neigh-boring churches.

PUPPET PLAYS

When students have become thoroughly familiar with a Bible story, they may choose to retell it in a puppet play. A good resource is Hand Puppets: How to Make and Use Them (see Bibliography). Cardboard stick puppets, hand puppets with paper-mache heads and cloth bodies, sock puppets, paper-bag hand or stick puppets, and many other kinds are possible. Shadowgraph puppets are also fun and easy to make.

Here's How:

1. Use an ordinary puppet stage except pull a white window shade over the open-ing or tape a piece of white muslin sheeting over the opening with masking tape. Light it from behind with an overhead projector, photographer's lamp, or gooseneck desk lamp. If you want to add color to the lighting effects, glue colored cellophane in cardboard frames large enough to hold in front of the source of light.

2. Obtain used X-ray film from a medical clinic or hospital. Clean the film in a well-ventilated room, using a solution of ½ cup chlorine bleach in 1 gallon of water. The black substance should come off easily after the films have soaked for a few minutes. Rub gently (so as not to scratch the film), rinse in clear water, and dry on a line or with paper towels. The clean film will have a bluish tint.

3. Have the students design their puppets on white drawing paper first and then lay the clean X-ray film over the drawings. Provide permanent black marking pens for them to use in tracing the outline and features of the puppets. They can add color with colored marking pens or acrylic paints, applied lightly with tiny brushes.

4. The students can cut out the puppets with scissors. The film tends to be somewhat brittle, but if it breaks can be repaired with transparent adhesive tape.

5. Use ¼-inch dowel sticks in 12-inch lengths as the sticks for the puppets. Attach them at a right angle to the puppets with thumbtacks.

6. The students can manipulate the puppets by pressing them against the shadowgraph screen from behind the stage. When the light shines from behind them, the shadows they cast on the screen will look like figures from a stained glass window.

CLASSROOM DRAMA

If the students decide to produce a classroom drama with live actors, a helpful resource is Twenty Ways to Use

Drama in Teaching the Bible (see Bibliography). In addition to the dramatic
forms described in that book, you
might suggest retelling the story in
the form of a radio or television
show, patterned after the "You Are
There" series of some years ago. The
"there" would be the setting and situation of the Bible story. For this
type of live dramatization (or for use
with puppets as described previously)
the students will have to develop a
script.

Here's How:

1. For this project, choose a strong,
action-filled, yet simple plot that
develops one major theme or concept.
This concept should be the theme for
your script.

2. With the student's help, list the
scenes in the story on individual cards.
Arrange them in proper sequence, and
identify the introduction, climax, and
conclusion.

3. On each of these cards, list the
characters for the scene. If you are
working with puppets, you will have to
consider how many characters can comfortably appear onstage at one time,
and plan accordingly. Remember to
allow room for the puppeteers backstage as well! If you are working with
a classroom drama, you may need to
adjust your characters to the number
of children who want to be in the play.
Usually, except for the major characters,
it is easy to make these adjustments.

4. Decide if and how you will use
narrative speeches as a bridge between
scenes, as a way of eliminating less
important scenes, or as a way of
explaining pantomimed scenes.

5. Decide what backgrounds and props
are essential and practical. Keep this
in mind as you plan.

6. Divide the students into writing
teams of no more than two or three
persons, or have them work individually.
Suggest that they choose which scenes

they want to write. Provide any
resources they will need: books,
pictures, Bibles, and so forth.

7. With the student's help, combine
the scenes into one script, editing
it as necessary. Consider: Does the
plot move along? Does the theme come
through clearly? Is the story logical?
Are the connecting narratives smooth?
Do the speeches have short, simple sentences that are easy to read and learn?

ART PROJECTS

Students who like to work in any of a
variety of art media may want to choose
one or more to use in retelling the
story in projects like these:
A mural is a large project, often
covering all or part of a wall, designed to be seen at a distance by
large groups of people. It may be done
as a whole or in sections to be taped
together later. It can involve painting,
drawing, collage, or printmaking.
A banner is a hanging, suspended from
the wall or ceiling, designed to create
a mood, speak a message, or tell a
story through words, symbols, designs,
and colors. Banners can come in all
shapes and sizes. Although they are
often made from burlap or felt, with
fabric appliques, they may also be
made from other materials such as
wrapping paper, transparent plastic,
nylon net, heavyweight nonwoven interfacing, or cardboard. Students can
use paints, fabric crayons, selfadhesive vinyl, magazine letters and
illustrations, wallpaper samples,
tissue paper in varied colors, and
colored construction paper to add
designs. Students can retell a story
in one large banner, or through a
series of smaller banners that can be
hung as a group.
Drawings in chalk, charcoal, or
crayons can be used to illustrate a
story. Students can choose different
scenes from the story to draw, mount
their drawings on posterboard, and

tape them together so they will fold
up like an accordion. This way they
will stand on a table for display.
 If you want to use art projects like
these with your students, consult a
resource like A Handbook of Arts and
Crafts (see Bibliography) for detailed,
illustrated directions for a variety
of art media.

SEE ALSO:

Kamishibai Theater
Student-Produced Visuals
New Texts for Old Tunes
Puppet Parade
Walking Bible Folk

A Workshop Design

Churches planning to encourage the use of this book may find it helpful to introduce it at a teachers' workshop such as the one described below. The workshop was designed to help teachers--

1. discuss their reasons for teaching Bible stories to children;

2. discover sixteen different categories of experiences that can help students learn a Bible story and relate it to their lives;

3. learn how to use at least one new teaching-learning activity within each category;

4. practice enriching a sample session plan with additional teaching-learning activities selected from three of the categories.

PUBLICITY

The form of publicity used would depend on whether the workshop is local or regional, denominational or ecumenical, in character. It should reach possible participants well in advance of the workshop and include the date, place, schedule, and what the teachers can expect to learn.

PHYSICAL ARRANGEMENTS AND EQUIPMENT

The room should be large enough to allow space for eight to ten learning centers, an open area for playing the get-acquainted game, and an area where three or four tables can be set up in a U-shape, with a blackboard, newsprint chart, or overhead projector and screen at the open end. There should be chairs for all the participants. Any audio-visual equipment to be used should be in good working order, with extension cords, spare bulbs, and extra batteries readily available.

If participants are from more than one congregation, there should be a registration table with name tags ready for everyone. Responsibilities for the meal (lunch or supper, depending on the schedule) should be assigned as soon as the workshop is scheduled.

SCHEDULE

20 minutes	Let's Get Acquainted
25 minutes	Brainstorming: What are some different kinds of experiences students can have that will help them

	learn a Bible story and relate it to their lives?
75 minutes	Paper Bag Surprise
45 minutes	Lunch/Supper
15 minutes	Browsing among Resources
60 minutes	More Experiences and Activities
30 minutes	How Does This Apply to Us?
15 minutes	Sharing Our Plans
15 minutes	Let's Celebrate in Worship

PROGRAM

Let's Get Acquainted

Prepare the picture cards as directed for the Bible Values Clarification Game (see Appendix 2). Proceed as indicated in the game directions until the teachers have shared what their cards have said to them about the Bible. Then ask each group to discuss: Why is it important for children to learn Bible stories? Have the groups write their ideas on pieces of newsprint and post them on the wall for all to see.

Brainstorming

Ask the teachers to move their chairs around the tables. Have copies of this book available, but do not distribute them until later. With one leader acting as recorder and the other as discussion leader, ask the group to think about this question: What are some different kinds of experiences students can have that will help them learn a Bible story and relate it to their lives? (If some teachers suggest specific teaching-learning activities, such as illustrating a scene from a story, reword the idea in terms of a category of experience, e.g., "seeing" the story or retelling the story.)
After the teachers have expressed their ideas, pass out copies of this book. Ask them to look at the table of contents to see if it suggests any other ideas to them. Add these to the list.
Then ask the teachers to consider the

list in terms of their own curriculum resources. Which of these categories of experience could be incorporated into their session plans? Would they be able to use all of them? Why or why not? (Probably the teachers will indicate (1) fewer kinds of experiences are possible with less complex stories, and (2) some of the experiences are more suited to one developmental stage than another.) Beginning with preschoolers and continuing through adults, ask the teachers to indicate which experiences are relevant to the different age groups. The recorder should indicate their choices by means of checkmarks in different colors. Point out that as the age of the students increases, so does the number of experiences that can help them learn a Bible story and relate it to their lives.
Explain that this book was written to enable church teachers to enrich their curriculum resources with additional teaching-learning activities designed to provide some of these experiences for their students. The rest of the workshop will give them a chance to participate in some activities selected from the book and consider how they might be used with a sample session plan.

PAPER BAG SURPRISE

Develop eight learning centers, each of which should provide a different experience that will help individuals or small groups learn a Bible story and relate it to their lives. Use a story from the participants' curriculum resources or select one at random. Set the centers up around the room.
For example, eight centers designed to provide experiences with the story of Paul's conversion in Acts 9 might be set up as follows:
1. Experience - *Where is it?*
   Activity - Bible Library Chart, Marked passages
2. Experience - *What is the story?*

Activity - Costumed storyteller or Bible storybooks with narration on cassette tape for a listening station.

3. Experience - *When did it happen?*
   Activity - Time line on a felt board, using symbols for Moses (stone tablets), David (crown), Jesus (cross), Paul (ship), and today (a child in modern dress). Have reference books available.

4. Experience - *Where did it happen?*
   Activity - Overhead projector with transparency of Mediterranean area drawn with permanent pens, so students can use nonpermanent pens to draw in a line between Jerusalem and Damascus and wipe off the line before the next student comes to the center.

5. Experience - *Want to know more?*
   Activity - Research, with these directions: Write a news release on the story, including this information: what Paul was doing in Jerusalem, why he was going to Damascus, who was with him, what happened, who came to help him and why. Sources: Acts 7:59-8:3; Bible dictionary and encyclopedia, s.v. Stephen, Saul, Paul, Ananias, Pharisee, persecute.

6. Experience - *What happened first?*
   Activity - Reconstructing a story from scrambled sentences.

7. Experience - *What do the words mean?*
   Activity - Pick-a-Picture Box with mounted pictures illustrating the concept of change. Discussion of how Paul was changed by his experience on the road to Damascus.

8. Experience - *What does God have to do with all this?*
   Activity - Opinion Box, with these directions: Pretend you are Paul, after your experience on the road to Damascus. Write your opinion about God's love, using this format: "I used to think God's love was _____ but now I know God's love is _____."

In each center, list the category of experience, the teaching-learning activity being used, and clear instructions for working with the resources there.

Give each person a small paper bag filled with tickets to each center, plus a few for fun (e.g., tell someone that he or she is your friend; eat a lemon drop; have a cup of coffee). Explain to the teachers that they are to draw out the tickets one at a time from their bags and work on the centers in that order. Establish a limit to the number of persons who can be in a center at one time. Suggest that if too many people draw out the same ticket simultaneously, some should put it back in their bags and draw another. When they have finished work in one center, they should move on to the next, provided there is room. Those who finish early may consult their copies of this book for additional teaching-learning activities listed under each category of experience.

BROWSING

If your library contains some of the resources listed in the Bibliography, display them at a table near the learning centers.

MORE EXPERIENCES AND ACTIVITIES

For this part of the program, choose experiences and related activities that may be shared by the teachers as a total group. For example:

1. Experience - *What do you see?*
   Activity - Kamishibai theater, prepared by the leader.

2. Experience - *What was that again?*
   Activity - Tic-Tac-Toe, using questions based on the story.

3. Experience - *Who plays what?*
   Activity - Who am I? Riddle rhymes for Saul/Paul, Ananias, Damascus Christians, Damascus Jews.

4. Experience - *Can you repeat that?*
   Activity - Paul's new message for

103

the world (Acts 9:20b - "He is the Son of God") in code.

5. Experience - *How is it spelled?*
   Activity - Spelling relay, using these words: Saul, Paul, Ananias, Jerusalem, Damascus.

6. Experience - *It's happening all over again!*
   Activity - Current Events: Search newspapers and magazines for examples of how persons today have turned their lives around in a new direction: persons with drug or alcohol problems who have become chemical dependency counselors for others, rehabilitated ex-convicts, business leaders who have entered the ministry or social service.

7. Experience - *How are they related?*
   Activity - Writing diamonte poems as a group on Saul/Paul.

8. Experience - *The story's worth telling again!*
   Activity - Write-on slides, with each person illustrating a different scene from the story.

HOW DOES THIS APPLY TO US?

Divide the teachers into groups according to the ages of the students they teach. Provide each group with a sample session plan for their age group, preferably one from a curriculum not being used by any of the participants. The plan should include a Bible story. Ask the teachers to read through the session plan, write down its main idea in their own words, and note how the story is used to teach that idea. Have them choose three categories of experiences that could be planned to help students learn this story and relate it to their lives. Then ask them to select a teaching-learning activity from each of the three categories and explain how they would incorporate the activities into the session plan.

SHARING OUR PLANS

Invite all the groups to share their suggestions for enriching this session plan with additional teaching-learning activities.

LET'S CELEBRATE IN WORSHIP

Incorporate some of the day's activities in an informal worship service; for example, the write-on slides, the decoded message, the opinions from the Opinion Box, or others. Close with a prayer and a fellowship hymn.

Appendix II
A Values Clarification Game

This is a game that gives individuals a chance to express their feelings and attitudes on issues, a theme, a controversial subject, or a thing. For example, the game may be used to explore what meaning the Bible has for people.

Here's How:

1. From magazines, cut out pictures, words, and slogans at random. Paste them on 5" x 8" cards, one to a card. Make about six cards per player.

2. To play the game, shuffle the cards and deal out five to each player. Ask the players to look at the cards and decide which ones best express their understanding of the Bible and its meaning to them. Explain that they should keep those cards, but can trade or discard the others. If there are more than ten players, have them trade their unwanted cards with one another. They may trade any number of cards at a time, so long as they trade one for one. If there are less than ten players, have them discard their unwanted cards and draw others from a reserve pile, one at a time. The cards in the discard pile should be laid face down so they can also be drawn. Players must have five cards in their hands at all times.

The trading period can last from five to ten minutes. At its end, ask the players to discard three of their cards, keeping the two cards that best express what the Bible means to them. Have the players share the cards they have kept and their reasons for keeping them. (If you are working with a large group, you may want to divide the players into smaller groups for this sharing time.)

Next, ask the group as a whole to consider the different meanings the Bible has for people today. List their responses on a newsprint chart, chalkboard, or overhead transparency. Encourage them to discuss briefly what this says about the Bible's relevancy to everyday life.

Finally, ask the group what experiences have had the greatest influence on their feelings about the Bible: church school, church worship, church fellowship groups, families, an individual, camp experiences? What does this say about the way the biblical faith is taught and learned?

Appendix III

Bibliography

BOOKS FOR STUDENT RESEARCH

Bible Encyclopedia for Children, by
 Cecil Northcott. Philadelphia:
 Westminister Press, 1964.
Golden Bible Atlas, by Samuel Terrien.
 Racine, Wis.: Golden Press, 1957.
Life in Bible Times, by Robert Henderson
 and Ian Gould; Mary Alice Jones, con-
 sultant editor. Chicago: Rand McNally
 & Co., 1967.
People of the Bible, by Cecil Northcott.
 Philadelphia: Westminister Press, 1967.
A Picture Book of Palestine, by Ethel
 L. Smither. Nashville: Abingdon, 1947.
A Picture Dictionary of the Bible, by
 Ruth P. Tubby. Nashville: Abingdon,
 1949.
A Picture Dictionary of Jewish Life, by
 Alvan D. Rubin. New York: Behrman
 House, Inc., 1956.
Young People's Bible Dictionary, by
 Barbara Smith. Philadelphia: West-
minister Press, 1965.
Young Reader's Bible. Nashville:
 Abingdon, 1965.
Young Reader's Dictionary of the Bible.
 Nashville: Abingdon, 1969.

SELF-INSTRUCTIONAL BIBLE STUDY

The Getting to Know Your Bible Series,
 by Paul B. and Mary Carolyn Maves.
Nashville: Graded Press, 1968-73.
Grades 4-6.
Finding Your Way Through the Bible is
designed to help children learn how
to look up Bible references and use
footnotes, maps, and study helps.
Learning More About Your Bible contains
general information about how and why
the books of the Bible are arranged in
a particular way.
Exploring How the Bible Came to Be
tells how the Bible grew out of
stories and songs to written records
accepted as sacred.
Discovering How the Bible Message
Spread describes how the Bible
spread around the world from the time
its list of books became official
until the present.

MEDIA RESOURCES

American Bible Society, 1865 Broadway,
 New York, New York 10023.
Better Media for Less Money, by Donn P.
 McGuirk. The Arizona Experiment, 1972.
Better Media Volume Two, by Donn P.
 McGuirk. The Arizona Experiment, 1978.
 Volumes 1 and 2 are available from
 National Teacher Education Project,
 6947 East MacDonald Drive, Scottsdale,
 Arizona 85253.

Bible Lands, Past and Present (1971)
and Bible Map Transparencies (1969).
Nashville: Broadman Films. Trans-
parencies for the overhead projector.
Church Teachers, an ecumenical peri-
odical with articles by and for
teachers, is published five times a
year. Order from National Teacher
Education Project, 6947 East MacDonald
Drive, Scottsdale, Arizona 85253.
Classroom Learning Centers, by John E.
Morlan et al. Belmont, Calif.:
Fearon, 1974. Available from Fearon
Publishers, 6 Davis Drive, Belmont,
California 94002.
Griggs Educational Service, 1731
Barcelona Street, Livermore, Cali-
fornia 94550, is a source for a
variety of resources. Write for a
catalog of resources including:
  Blank playing cards, approximately
  seventy to a pack
  Write-on slides and write-on
  filmstrips
  Overhead transparencies and pens
  Picture-lift plastic
  Slide mounts
  Biblical simulation games and
  activities
  Scripture Cards, produced by the
  American Bible Society (approximately
  thirty cards with Good News Bible line
  drawings on one side and scripture
  passages on the other, plus an instruc-
  tion sheet with suggestions for using
  the cards)
A Handbook of Arts and Crafts for
Elementary and Junior High School, by
Willard F. Wankelman and Phillip Wigg.
4th ed. rev. Dubuque, Iowa: William
C. Brown Co., 1978.
More Puppets with Pizazz: Fifty
Rod, Novelty, and String Puppets
Children Can Make and Use, by
Joy Wilt, Gwen Hurn, and John
Hurn. Waco, Texas: Creative
Resources, 1977.

DRAMA RESOURCES

Faith Alive is a series of fifteen-
minute dramatizations of Bible stories,
originally recorded for radio by the
United Church of Canada. Available
from THESIS, Box 11724, Pittsburgh,
Pennsylvania 15228.
Hand Puppets: How to Make and Use Them
by Laura Ross. Lothrop, Lee, and
Shepard Co., 1969.
That I May Speak: Rhythmic Speech
Ensembles, by Betty Ann Ramseth.
Minneapolis: Augsburg, 1970.
Twenty Ways to Use Drama in Teaching
the Bible, by Judy Gattis Smith.
Livermore, Calif.: Griggs Educational
Service, 1975.

MUSIC RESOURCES

Choristers Guild Letters, published
monthly (September through June) by
Choristers Guild, Box 38188, Dallas,
Texas 75238. The monthly packets
include suggestions for using biblical
material in choral speaking, inter-
pretive movement, anthems, hymns,
banners, dramatized musicals, and other
teaching-learning activities in the
church, especially those related to
music.
Rejoice and Sing Praise: A Collection
of Songs and Materials to be Used with
Elementary Boys and Girls, compiled by
Evelyn Andre and Jeneil Menefee; Myron
Braun, musical consultant. Nashville:
Abingdon, 1977.

DRAMATIZED MUSICALS: SCORES AND RECORDINGS

A Night for Dancing, by Hal H. Hopson,
Dallas: Choristers Guild, 1974. Based
on Luke 2:8-20.
David and the Giants, by Albert Zabel
and Trilby Jordan. Dallas: Choristers
Guild, 1975. Based on I Samuel 17.
It's Cool in the Furnace, by Buryl Red
and Grace Hawthorne. Waco, Tex.: Word
Music, Inc., 1973. (Recorded on WORD
Records-WST-8580.) Based on Daniel 1-3.

Jonah's Tale of a Whale, by Robert
  Graham and Jeana Graham. Nashville:
  Broadman Press, 1974. (Recorded on
  Broadman Album 4585-17.) Based on
  Jonah 1-3.
Joseph and the Amazing Technicolor
  Dreamcoat, by Andrew Lloyd Webber
  and Time Rice. New York: Belwin Mills
  Publishing Corp., 1969. Abridged
version published by Novello & Co.
  Ltd, distributed by Belwin Mills.
  (Recorded on Decca LK/SKL 4973.) Based
  on Genesis 37-50.
100% Chance of Rain: A Jazz Cantata
  for Young Singers, by Walter S.
  Horsley. Dallas: Choristers Guild,
  1972. Based on Genesis 6-9.

Index